On the Road With a Circus

(Illustrated Edition)

by

W. C. Thompson

The Echo Library 2020

Published by

The Echo Library

Echo Library
Unit 22
Horcott Industrial Estate
Horcott Road
Fairford
Glos. GL7 4BX

www.echo-library.com

Please report serious faults in the text to complaints@echo-library.com

ISBN 978-1-84702-360-5

On the Road
With a Circus

by

W. C. THOMPSON

NEW YORK

NEW AMSTERDAM BOOK COMPANY

1905

Copyright, 1903,
By W. C. THOMPSON

Copyright, 1905,
By NEW AMSTERDAM BOOK COMPANY

EAGER THRONG AT THE MAIN ENTRANCE.

TABLE OF CONTENTS.

CHAPTER I
    THE MODERN CIRCUS..8

CHAPTER II
    ARRIVAL AND DEBARKATION 19

CHAPTER III
    EARLY SCENES ON THE LOT 26

CHAPTER IV
    THE PARADE 33

CHAPTER V
    THE SIDE-SHOW 38

CHAPTER VI
    AT THE MAIN ENTRANCE 47

CHAPTER VII
    THE MENAGERIE TENT 54

CHAPTER VIII
    LIFE WITH THE PERFORMERS 61

CHAPTER IX
    NIGHT SCENES AND EMBARKATION 75

CHAPTER X
    THE CIRCUS DETECTIVE 80

CHAPTER XI
    THE AUTOBIOGRAPHY OF A CIRCUS HORSE.....................83

CHAPTER XII
    THE CIRCUS BAND *BY BANDMASTER WILLIAM MERRICK*................88

CHAPTER XIII
    WITH THE ELEPHANTS 91

CHAPTER XIV
    THE GENERAL MANAGER 99
CHAPTER XV
    AMERICAN CIRCUS TRIUMPHANT 104
CHAPTER XVI
    THE OLD-FASHIONED CIRCUS 113
CHAPTER XVII
    THE CIRCUS PRESS AGENT 121

LIST OF ILLUSTRATIONS

EAGER THRONG AT THE MAIN ENTRANCE. *(Frontispiece)* 4
CIRCUS ENCAMPMENT AT EARLY DAWN. 16
DISEMBARKING FROM THE CIRCUS TRAIN. 24
CIRCUS COOKS PREPARING BREAKFAST. 28
TWO HEN'S EGGS, HAMMER, FILE AND NAIL-CLAW PRESENTED
    BY A PLEADING, PENNILESS MISSISSIPPI NEGRO BOY TO SECURE
    ADMISSION. HE GOT IN. 31
BAREBACK RIDERS READY FOR THE RING. 42
BEFORE THE CROWD COMES. 49
A "MAN KILLER," PHOTOGRAPHED HALF AN HOUR AFTER
    HAVING SLAIN AN ANNOYER. 55
REHEARSING IN WINTER QUARTERS. 57
RING "STARS" LINED UP FOR INSPECTION. 63
PRACTISING TRICKS IN THE OPEN. 70
PERFORMERS AT THEIR MIDDAY MEAL. 76
TEACHING HER HORSE NEW TRICKS. 84
ELEPHANT HERD "AT ATTENTION." 92
ELEPHANTS "WORKING THEIR WAY." 97
TRANSFERRING FROM WATER TO RAIL. 110
HUMILIATION OF THE KING OF BEASTS. 115
FAIR EQUESTRIENNE ON HER FAVORITE HORSE. 122
ACROBATS PRACTISING NEW FEATS. 128

ON THE ROAD WITH A CIRCUS

CHAPTER I

THE MODERN CIRCUS

The faithful recording of daily life with one of the "big shows," wandering with it under all vicissitudes, fortunate or adverse, is the errand on which this book is sent. You and I will travel from the distraction and tumult of the summer season to the congenial quiet of winter quarters, and survey operations from the hour when new and unwonted scenes and sounds startle city quiet or country seat retirement until the stealthy breaking of the white encampment and the departure from town. We will scrutinize the entrance of strangers into strange lands and observe the rising and expansion of the tents as an army of men stamp their image upon the earth. Our astonished eye will gaze upon the gorgeous pageant of the parade and returning to the grounds will peer freely and familiarly about the place of strange sounds and entrancing sights. We will watch the master mind of the circus and his associates in counsel and action. We will study the life, character, and habits of the motley throng of "show" people and learn of morals and manners, of hopes and fears, of trials and solicitudes; and we will pass sunny hours on meadows enamelled with violets and daisies and goldened with buttercups and dandelions, where the circus is passing its day.

We circus people have so high an opinion of our good qualities that we are not ashamed to introduce ourselves to you. As pilgrims with no abiding city, leading a life of multiplied activities and varied fortunes amid scenes of din and turmoil, hurry and agitation, our platform is courage, ambition, and energy, governed by honest purpose and tempered by humanity. We have our infirmities, our faults, and our sins, but also our virtues, our excellences, and our standards of perfection, and a discerning world has come no longer to regard us as unscrupulous invaders, but as invited and welcome guests. The voice of joy and health resounds through our ranks; we are united in fraternal good-will unbroken by dissension, our life of weal and woe is ever invested with peculiar delightful fascination, and boisterous relish transports itself from town to town. Memory clings with fond tenacity to halcyon days with the circus.

Sometime between 1820 and 1830 (circus annals tell not exactly the year), near what is now New York City, while a red-coated band blew forth a merry melody, a round-top tent swelled upward. The parents of some of the present-day performers remember the day. It was the first cloth circus shelter erected in this country, and then what was formerly an open-air show assumed the dignity and importance of an under-cover performance. A crude enough affair it was, as compared with the perfection and finish of the modern circus. The flags and streamers and bunting which add grace and beauty waved no friendly greeting; the clamorous welcome of side-show orators and ticket sellers was wanting; no menagerie offered its accumulated wealth of curious and snarling beasts; human curiosity had not been awakened by the overpowering splendor and magnificence of a preliminary parade; there was a lack of sentiment and excitement and appeal to the senses; only din and confusion and broiling heat. From this mean beginning has come the marvellous circus of to-day, involving a business so extensive that few people possess anything but the vaguest conception of its magnitude, organization, and methods of operation.

Underlying the pomp and glitter and the odor of sawdust and naphtha is a system of government and management whose scale and scope are stupendous and staggering. No human institution is more perfect in operation and direction. Surely no more flattering tribute could be paid than that officially given us by the United States Government. Officers from the army department, skilled veterans in their profession, critically observed the swift sequence of proceedings when we showed in Washington—the early arrival of the trains; the rapid debarkation; the magical growth of the white encampment; the parade passing with measured tread through deeply lined streets; the scene on the grounds and at the performances, and the pulling down at night and the hurried, though orderly, departure. Then Gen. Nelson A. Miles surveyed the scene and expressed wonder and admiration. Finally there came a request that two representatives of the department be permitted to accompany the circus for two weeks. To the Government had come a realization that the modern circus offered lessons in the transportation and handling of men and horses, canvas and vehicles. And when the Barnum & Bailey Show was in Europe, the monarch of one of the world-powers, visiting under tents incognito, confessed that he had profited immensely by what he had witnessed, and proposed to put into immediate effect many of the original working arrangements of the circus. For instance, astonished at the ease and celerity with which the heavy circus wagons were run on to the cars by means of a block and tackle and an inclined plane, he admitted, ruefully, that in his vast army they had been hoisting their artillery over the sides of the cars. It remained for the American circus to bring appreciation of the waste of time and labor.

So to the humble employee of the circus who wanders with it from place to place, one day in one town and the next perhaps one hundred miles distant for a period of more than thirty weeks, is a part of the strange daily life, witnesses the emergencies constantly met and dealt with and the perplexing obstacles overcome, comes a forcible and convincing knowledge that it is not an ungodly thing to be questioned and looked at askance, but a genial, legitimate, business enterprise, based upon sound principles and conducted upon the highest lines of ability and responsibility by men who assumed a risk at which the nerviest professional gambler would hesitate. The amount of capital invested is several million dollars; no insurance company will give protection. The dangers of the road are never absent. A cataclysm of damage suits is a constant peril. Rainy weather, preventing performance and profit, may be a companion for months. There must be constant renewal of costly perishable property. Deaths of costly rare animals may swallow up the receipts of days. Continual other dangers and losses, of whose frequency, gravity, and magnitude the general public has no adequate conception, are encountered. Against these ruining possibilities the circus stakes.

There is a popular misapprehension regarding the profits of the circus business. Some of the large organizations have continued in existence for periods of several years without returning a cent on the investment or at an actual operating loss. Less strongly financed tented shows succumb. The circus is an infallible register of the monetary condition of the country. Hard times are reflected in it, and prosperity fills it with joyous evidence. The daily expenses of our circus are placed by the management at over $5,000, and a moment's calculation discloses that the receipt of this amount of money is not the quick operation surface conditions often indicate. The average daily free admissions are eleven hundred. These are largely the tickets given for bill-posting privileges. This territory embraces, generally, forty miles on the lines of all converging railroads and a distance of twenty miles in both directions from the tracks. City officials, newspapers, and a throng of others claim the remaining gratuitous entrance passes. Sometimes the number is larger. In one city we have been obliged to place three thousand free tickets.

Experienced circus owners reckon that one-quarter of the attendance comprises children under nine years of age and who pay half-rate, twenty-five cents. Thus it will be seen that some thirteen thousand persons, including those with free tickets, must pass the door each day before a dollar's profit has been yielded from this source for the management. Our "big top's" capacity is ten thousand persons. One realizes, after consideration of these facts and figures, how necessary it is that there be few vacant seats at either performance to insure a profit for the day, and how often the net revenue is supplied entirely by side-show, peanuts, popcorn, lemonade, and other small departments. Moreover, when the casual observer convinces himself that the huge tent is full to repletion, he is often badly mistaken. The circus usher must perform his duty with great care and systematic thoroughness, else he will permit the man who has paid for one seat to occupy two or more.

The circus does not run its season, dissolve, and disperse. In winter the entire establishment is maintained. Only the performers and workmen are dropped, and with the former this is generally a mere suspension of service, for contracts are frequently made for several years. Owners, managers, contracting agents, advertising agents, press agents, treasurer, bookkeepers, and others, find no idle moments. Rolling stock, suffering from the hard effects of a season's campaign, needs painter and carpenter; new acts and novelties must be secured to keep abreast of the times; the new route must be laid out and considered; and to do this the management must know the population and character of every town; have information of the condition of business, vicissitudes of the year and the prospects for the coming season; know the national, state, and municipal law and the character of licenses, and the price of food for man and beast; keep track of floods, droughts, or disasters to crops or people; be conversant with the periods of ploughing and harvesting; learn what railroads run in and out of town, their grades and condition, the extent, strength, and height of tunnels and bridges and the relative positions of railroad yards and the show lot; and find out the condition of the soil wherever the circus is booked in case of rain, and provide in advance for such a contingency. The circus is a fair-weather show and the management must have a definite knowledge of wet and dry seasons, to avoid encountering, so far as human foresight is possible, unpropitious meteorological conditions.

The question of transportation is the most careful one involved, and upon its cost and facilities the route of the circus is in a great measure determined. For instance, up in agricultural Windsor county, in southeastern Vermont, nestles the village of White River Junction. It boasts a weekly newspaper, a public school, and a national and a savings bank. Its population does not exceed fifteen hundred; yet the big circuses make annual pilgrimages thither because it is a local trade centre, the Boston and Maine, Central Vermont and Woodstock railroads converge upon it, and there the White and Connecticut rivers merge their waters. Its selection for exhibition purposes is a good illustration of the important part transportation facilities play in arranging routes. White River Junction itself would not turn out patrons enough to pay for the menagerie's food, but the throngs conveyed there by train and boat always fill the tents. So it is all over the country, barring the large cities. It is not so much the character and size of the place picked for the tents as its topographical position and drawing powers.

All through the winter a corps of women is busy on new uniforms and trappings for man, woman, and beast. There are rich plush and gold bullion galore in this workshop. The pretty spangles that will glitter in the ring are being sewed in place, the elephants are getting new jackets of royal purple and gold, and the camels are being fitted out afresh for the parade. Some of these gorgeous fittings are very expensive, but the circus management calculates that they must be renewed every year. The outlay for hats, boots, and other articles of attire for the army is heavy and ceaseless.

Circus day, to the men who have hundreds of thousands of dollars invested, it will be seen, means the culmination of long and careful and systematic preparation. To get ready for the day has been the work of many months and has employed the talents and attention of men wonderfully expert in their particular fields. The advance staff of one of the "big shows" usually consists of a general agent, a railway contractor, an executive agent, several general contracting agents, and assistants; car No. 1, carrying eighteen to twenty persons; first regular advertising car No. 2, bearing the chief press agent, car manager, and from twenty to twenty-five men; car No. 3, with eighteen to twenty men; car No. 4, carrying a special press agent and car manager and from twelve to fourteen men, including "route riders" and special ticket agents; next and finally, the "layer-out," who is one day ahead of the circus.

The railroad contractor is the first man out. He is familiar to the finest details with every railroad in the country—its mileage, connections, yard facilities, bridges and tunnels. He plans, besides arranging for the transportation of the circus trains, the special excursions which will converge upon the town on the specified day of exhibition. The general contracting agent follows. He makes contracts for feed, lot, accommodations for advance men, livery teams, and billboards. The contracts of these two men involve many thousands of dollars every week and must pass the rigid scrutiny of the experienced general agent. No detail of the business is unfamiliar to him.

Car No. 1 is professionally known as the "skirmishing car." It is most frequently called into service to fight opposition. As soon as a railway contractor of a rival circus puts in an appearance on the route the general manager is promptly notified. There is at once a formidable concentration of forces at the threatened point. No stone is left unturned or chance overlooked to gain an advantage; and the circus man is resourceful of schemes and plots. Billboards, barns, fences, hedges, trees, windows, and all other available space is bought up with apparently reckless expenditures. Banners, printed on muslin, are swung from walls and awnings. Sometimes more money than will be realized on show day is spent in this fight for publicity, but the circus regrets not a cent of it if the opposition has been taught a lesson and will not venture again to cross the path.

Attached to a passenger train and about four weeks ahead of the show, comes car No. 2. The general contracting press agent is aboard with his advertising cuts and prepared advertising matter, or keeping pace with it on the route. Sometimes there is a steam calliope, which produces marvellous sonorific effects at sundown, to the dismay of all who live in the immediate neighborhood, but calling obtrusive attention to the approach of the circus. The force of men bills and lithographs for miles around. Each team has a native driver who knows every road and every inhospitable bulldog. Permission is always secured from the owner or lessee of the spot selected for decoration, for without his consent, the astute showman knows, a poster becomes soon a thing of shreds and tatters. In return for the privilege an order is given on the circus for tickets, which is promptly honored if the agreement has been honestly kept.

The men on two other cars see to it that the work of their predecessors is followed up carefully. Various neglected preliminary work is in their charge. They replace posters torn down or mutilated and try to find new points of advantage. They check up and report every discrepancy of the other advance men, too, and send a detailed report to the general agent. The last man before the arrival of the circus is the "layer-out" or "twenty-four-hour man." He inspects the lot, fixes the route of the procession, and performs a variety of other final duties.

Sometimes a stereopticon man is sent out, but not unless there is opposition or the outlook for the day's business is bad. He stretches a big white sheet on a popular corner and entertains the town for an evening, adroitly advertising the show and putting the people in good humor.

A general agent estimates for me that the score of pretentious circuses employ, during at least seven months of the year, an average of fifty bill-posters each, making a total of six hundred men, outside of agents, contractors, inspectors, etc. To properly transport, supply, and provide for these employees it requires not less than thirty-six advertising cars, which, in the course of a season, cover every part of the American continent and the better part of Europe. These men post upward of one hundred and seventy thousand sheets of paper daily, and as their display of paper usually has a thirty days' showing for each day's exhibition, it is safe to estimate that from five millions to five millions two hundred thousand sheets are in sight for six months of the year. To-day the public often measures the value of an enterprise largely by the size and character of its posters. The development of poster printing and bill posting is due largely to the demands of the circus. Not all the commercial advertisers put together use posters so liberally as do the combined circus interests. The requirements of the circus built the boards and the results obtained forced the business to become a permanent and recognized factor in active commercial life.

One big circus used in a season seventy-seven kinds of posters, varying in size from one to sixty sheets and let loose on the public twelve publications, from a four-sheet to a twenty-page courier. They had a total edition of five million four hundred thousand copies.

The elevated standard of morality among circus men and women is a revelation to one who lives with them from day to day and is their close companion. The atmosphere and environment seem charged with health and happiness, virtue and vigor. Drunkenness is not tolerated in any form. Immediate discharge, no matter who or what the rank of the offender, is its penalty, and except in isolated instances among the canvasmen there is seldom provocation for punishment. Of other vices which are prevalent in many walks of life there is no evidence. The very nature of the business, with its claims on brain and body, forbids immoral or vicious excesses. Those who indulge in them are looked upon with coldness by their associates and made to feel themselves delinquents. Gambling is strictly prohibited, and fines are imposed upon the employee who is heard using profane or vulgar language. The women of the circus are not permitted even to engage in conversation with any one not directly connected with the show. Most of them spend a few hours each Sunday in church. A fine awaits the luckless man caught exchanging words with an outside woman. It is the effort and aim of the management, too, to inculcate a spirit of good-fellowship and enduring affection, founded upon mutual respect and esteem. It demands that all be obliging and civil, answer questions politely, assist patrons in distress, smooth ruffled tempers, in short, make people who go to the circus feel at home, have a good time, and want to come again.

Circus folk, like sailors, are perhaps the most superstitious people in the world. They have numerous curious beliefs and all possess pet superstitions. Disease, disaster and death are presaged in their minds by signs and wonders. Few are without amulets and charms. Four-leafed clovers, made as pendants in silver or glass, and rabbits' feet set in silver are favorites to ward off evil. Many have horseshoes nailed to their trunks for luck. To see three white horses in succession and no red-headed woman is a forerunner of good luck. So, too, they declare, is the sight of a boxed corpse in a railroad station as the train rolls in. It is an ill omen to catch a glimpse of the death receptacle when leaving a town. Tapping a hunchback on his hump is sure to result favorably, and a white speck showing on the finger nail indicates auspicious things. The appearance of a white foamy spot on the surface of a cup of coffee or tea denotes "money," and should be at once swallowed intact. To open an umbrella in a house is sure to result in a shower of trouble, and one's future is risked by going under a ladder. Breaking a mirror is significant of death and seven years' ill-luck. If undergarments are put on wrong side out, it is tempting fate to change them until removed for the night. A peacock's presence is fraught with promise of dire evil, and a stuffed bird or a fan of its feathers bodes ill for the owner. To eat while a bell is tolling for a funeral will bring misfortune. The hooting of owls at night is ominous of death. Bad luck may be expected if a mouse gnaws a gown. To rock an empty cradle will entail injury to the child who should occupy it. Salt spilt at the table is a warning of a quarrel, unless a pinch of the mineral is promptly thrown over the right shoulder. Stray cats have their terrors, but a black one is welcome.

Many performers invariably go into the ring putting the right foot forward. If they neglect to do this they back out and re-enter. All believe a cross-eyed man should never be permitted inside, the tents; evil times accompany him. Few foreigners fail to cross themselves before performing, and nearly all wear strange charms. Many circus people regard a color or a combination of colors as a hoodoo. None would venture to cross a funeral, and I have seen those who turn their backs until a death procession has passed out of sight and hearing. All believe Friday an unlucky day, and are sure there are fortunate and unfortunate hours in every day. If Friday falls on the thirteenth day of a month, it will bring misfortune, for thirteen cuts a wide swath in the profession.

In marked contrast to the popular notions of the rank and file of circus men is the practice of Mr. James A. Bailey, who founds his business conduct along lines tending to discourage superstition. Friday is his accepted choice upon which to make an important move—the Barnum & Bailey show left America on Friday—and he welcomes the figure 13 in any transaction. His marvellously successful career perplexes credulous associates.

The slang and colloquialisms of the circus form a secret language in themselves, a collection of jargon, racy, pungent, and pregnant of meaning, and always used in familiar conversation. "Stall," as noun or verb, is a popular and widely employed expression. It indicates anything tending to conceal real intention, a confederate who diverts attention, an accomplice under cover. For instance, "I am stalling for a walkaway," if I refrain from notifying a customer that he has forgotten his change. The "walkaway," a flurried, absent-minded, or hurrying person who leaves his return money behind, is legion and a constant source of joy to the ticket-seller. "Nix" is a significant circus watchword, whose utterance generally is the signal announcing the approach of some one in authority or who is not a confidant. It is used, too, as the curt form of request to desist from word or deed. The exhibition place is never anything but a "lot" in circus parlance, and the organization itself is referred to as the "show." A "snack-stand" is the improvised structure at railroad depot or show ground where a hasty bite of food can be obtained. The men who sell candy, popcorn, lemonade and the like are "butchers." The tents are "tops" in the circus vocabulary. The canvas under which the performance is given is known as the "big top," the eating tent as the "cook top," and so on. One might travel a season with a circus and not hear the word tent mentioned. The side-show is the "kid show," as the vernacular of the profession has it.

Employees are "working" whether driving stakes, throwing somersaults, or sitting on exhibition as a curiosity. The broad license of the word is amusing to the stranger who hears the Albino, whose sole occupation is to receive the stares of side-show visitors, remark that "she didn't work yesterday," but remained in the car all day. The rallying-cry, "Hey Rube!" has become a vague memory among modern circuses. Ample police protection is assured nowadays, the character of circus employees is higher and the discipline is sterner, and the days of sanguinary encounters among themselves or with town rowdies are gone forever. The inaugural procession around the tent is the circus man's "tournament." A "grafting" show is the circus with dishonest motives, as described in another chapter, and its "fixer" or "squarer" is the man who makes the corrupt arrangement with town officials. In circus dialect "yap" and "simp" indicate a credulous rustic who is easy prey for sharpers.

The policeman in plain clothes is rather contemptuously referred to as a "flattie." A trunk is known as a "keester" and a valise as a "turkey." Circus dialect for a man is always "guy," and the proprietor of the show is invariably styled "the main guy," or the "main squeeze." The former appellation is probably adapted from the fact that the main guy rope holds the tent in position. To "fan a guy" is to make an examination to discover whether or not he is carrying concealed weapons. A pocketbook is a "leather," a watch a "super," and a watch chain a "slang." "Lid" signifies a hat and a ticket is called a "fake." A complimentary ticket or a railroad pass has no other name than "brod." An elephant in circus language is never anything except a "bull." The showman's word for peanuts is "redhots," and their lemonade concomitant is designated "juice." "Plain juice" is water. Human eyes are "lamps," and heads are chosen "nuts."

The posters and lithographs sent out in advance are "paper," and the programmes and other literature are distinguished as "soft stuff." Side-show orators have the cognomens "spielers" and "blowers," and the employee who has charge of the naphtha torches, which are "beacons" in the circus world, is known as the "chandelier man." Reserved seats are alluded to as "reserved," and all other allotted sitting space is termed "the blues," derived from the painted color of the boards. Clowns are "joys" and the other performers "kinkers."

The history of the circus records many disasters by fire, wind, and wreck, but only a few solitary instances in which patrons have suffered. In none of the vocations of life, in times of crisis, are given better examples of energy, daring, discipline, and power of command and obedience. For more than a score of years, since the old method of overland horse and wagon mode of transportation was abandoned for the swift, modern steam-engine way, hardly a year has failed to catalogue a catastrophe entailing loss of life and property and human and animal misery. Yet death and damage are confined to the ranks of the show people.

CIRCUS ENCAMPMENT AT EARLY DAWN.

Railroads are notoriously indifferent to the interests of the long, heavy circus trains in their temporary keeping. Accidents in transit are frequent. A misplaced switch, confusion in running schedules, a careless engineer or trainman, may bring impoverishing adversity. The circus is never exempt from peril, when planted for the day in apparent security, when journeying from town to town or when housed in wood or brick. Misfortune follows, too, even to winter quarters, where, perhaps, general impression assumes to the circus owner freedom from care and apprehension. There are many things conspiring to make him old before his time.

The Southern States generally yield good profits, but the crowds are more disorderly, often, than in any other section of the country. Guns protrude from many pockets and their owners are eager for a chance to brandish or discharge them. Inflamed by whiskey, these circus visitors are a constant menace to life and property. It is only by an exercise of great diplomacy that we escape frequent trouble. Mississippi is greatly accredited among showmen with being the most dangerous State in the Union, as is the police force of Philadelphia called the most efficient for their purposes. The New York bluecoats are called upon for little display of their ability and organization with the circus established in the stone and wood of Madison Square Garden. Municipal officers throughout the South have the reputation, whether justified or not, of being past grand masters in the subtle art of "shake-down," the circus man's parlance for palpably unfair means of extracting money. Extortionate fees are levied for all privileges, and in many cities hordes of professional damage seekers await a pretense of excuse for demanding money.

In one city, for instance, the owner of the land on which we exhibited gave plain directions as to its area and they were abided by. At eleven o'clock, when all the preliminary work of the day had been performed, his neighbor rushed to the lot and demanded four hundred dollars; his property, a worthless patch of rocky soil, had been encroached upon six feet by one end of the "big top!" It was a frank attempt at extortion and the native nursed the conviction that the circus was powerless to do aught but pay. Little did he imagine the resourceful energy of the showman in a crisis! Under the owner's personal supervision, the big reaches of canvas were levelled again, while the landholder stood by in amazement. At noon, an hour and a half after the unreasonable demand, the circus had moved itself the required distance and taught the Southerner a lesson he will not forget.

The incident is an example of the deliberate purpose of many persons to take unfair advantage of the circus and illustrates how completely their nefarious plans sometimes go awry.

Trouble came unceasing that same day. The crowd was ugly and seeking fight, and some of its members even invaded the rings and insulted performers. We were told that night that ours was the only circus that ever left town without undergoing the annoyance of having the side ropes cut, a playful prank of the place. On the night journey from lot to cars, the hippopotamus cage tipped over and was righted with great difficulty, while the huge inmate roared his fright and disapproval. Later, the big vehicle conveying the side-show paraphernalia collapsed near the same spot and made more work and delay, and filled the roughs with glee at our plight. The colored "snack stand" proprietors, who, of course, are no part of the show, were robbed of their proceeds by native thieves, amid great wailing, and a colored man was killed by the cars in the confusion at the loading place. The circus men were the only witnesses to rush to him in the hope of giving relief. Never were men, women, and children happier over a change of scene than when our trains moved to new environments.

During the night run, a desperate attempt was made to rob the money wagon. Two men were busily working with brace and bit and hammer and saw, when the watchman, patrolling his lonely beat along the line of cars, came upon them. They jumped from the slow-moving train and escaped in the darkness.

The well-organized circus seldom misses a performance. Rain and mud are its enemies, but their combined endeavors only infrequently prevent erection of tents, and the parade and exhibition which then infallibly follow. There are instances in which the elements have upset plans for two or three successive days, but conditions are seldom so unkind. Shovel and pickaxe and beds of absorbing straw accomplish wonders. If denied the opportunity to erect the "big top," sometimes the show is given in the less expansive menagerie tent and the animal cages are kept on the cars. The enforced arrangement is unsatisfactory to circus man and patron, but to the former it gives the consolation that the day will not be entirely without receipts.

The recuperative powers of the circus are marvellous. Many a show which has been almost entirely exterminated by a railroad wreck or other disaster has within a few weeks again taken up the thread of dates. The reason for this quick restoration is that duplicates of almost every necessity can be obtained. A hurry call brings a new tent to replace the damaged one. Men who make a business of supplying circus menageries with animals ship a great new variety at once, and in an incredibly short time the renewed show is on the move once more.

CHAPTER II

ARRIVAL AND DEBARKATION

Through the gloom of night and the dusk of early morning the heavy circus train labors on its journey to transient destination. The distance diminishes slowly. Sometimes the line of cars is shunted to one side and stands patient and inert while expresses clatter by; again, its dragging weight defies the straining efforts of the engine, and it is left in solitary helplessness while the iron horse scurries off for aid; often the cars are rattled together with body-racking violence. Farmers in the barnyards rub their eyes in mute astonishment at the moving spectacle, and cattle scamper from fright. Other trains are in hot pursuit. Their burden, too, is man and beast and varied showy paraphernalia. Four or five sections are required to transport the vast and wondrous effects of the circus.

A quiet, unpretending village has already begun to assume an air of stir and animation. Festal circus day is at hand. Parents and children line the railroad approach and eagerly seize upon all points of vantage. Keen curiosity and joyful anticipation are depicted on every face. The railroad yards are empty of rolling stock, and switchmen and engines are ready to receive and admit the travelling pageant and pilot it to a place convenient to its needs. No preparatory arrangement that human foresight can conceive has been neglected.

The intuitive welcoming shouts of boys and girls, a blurred slender outline in the distance, the screeching of railway whistles and the hurried orders of officials. Then a pressure of brakes, a crunching of wheels and a rattle of coupling pins. The circus has arrived!

One of the first to alight is the circus mail-carrier, who hurries off to the post-office. Important mail may await his coming and there must be no delay in its delivery. This is the first of three trips to the government station he will make that day, and between these journeys, which are frequently long and tedious, he will perform a variety of other work allotted to him at the lot. He knows by name every employee of the show, and his prompt and accurate service is rewarded at the close of each season with a purse of contributed money which invariably approaches a thousand dollars. At his heels is the general manager whose multifarious duties require early rising. The circus detective follows behind, scrutinizing faces and figures, conferring with railroad officials and approaching by easy stages the local police station. There are two sleeping-cars carrying performers and business staff on the first section. A great brushing of clothes and final completion of toilet, performed generally on the car platforms, precede their departure from the railroad yards.

The first section is known as the "baggage train." It bears the paraphernalia necessary to the immediate wants of the encampment, as follows: stake and chain wagons, canvas wagons, side-pole and centre-pole wagons, side-show wagon, stable wagons, water-tank wagons, cook-tent and blacksmith wagons, chandelier wagon, about two hundred draft horses, all dressing-room necessities except the trunks, the two performers' and business staff's sleeping-cars and the cars of most of the workingmen and their horses.

In the second train are jack wagon, the tableaux wagons, the elephants and camels and their keepers, performing, ring and baggage horses, seat and stringer wagons, "property" wagons, and all the appliances for performers and their baggage. The third and other sections carry more sleeping-cars and all the cages.

Twenty-two horses are allotted to each stock car. There are animals of all kinds and colors and sizes, from the saucy ponies and fleet, slender chariot beasts to the big, white ring and the heavily harnessed draft horses. The circus carries close to half a thousand of these equines. They are so loaded that they must needs stand erect during the journey, for injury and perhaps death, experience has taught, is the inevitable result of one of the brutes disposing himself, by accident or design, in any other position. The packing of them so close together that the possibility of this disaster is precluded is a duty delegated to the "wedge horse" of each car. After every other animal has taken his accustomed place at night and when to the lay observer they are as tightly compressed as safety demands, the trained "wedge horse" scampers up the inclined plane and burrows his way between the two animals in the centre of the car. He shoves and pushes until he is accommodated, and not until then is the boss hostler satisfied that there will be no accident. Although it would appear that they are crowded to unnecessary extreme, the circus man understands that the compression in reality renders the railroad trip more comfortable, for the wrenches and jars incidental to the journey have far less deleterious effect upon them than would be the case if they were loosely loaded.

Each driver has his team of two, four, six, eight, or ten horses and he makes two trips to the exhibition ground. Each wagon has its number, and each day and night the same man and beasts have it in charge. The drivers seem to have an intuitive knowledge of topography. Often the lot is several miles distant from the place of arrival and unloading, but these men of the reins are never confused as to locality or direction. They make the most complicated journeys without hesitation or mistake, seldom resorting to interrogating the native residents. Roads curve and wind in a manner most bewildering, but they keep steadily toward the scene of exhibition. These rides through pretty suburban streets in the gray light of the morning are often very delightful and invigorating. Generally, sidewalks are lined and porches packed with people eager to get their first glance of the circus, though its beauty and grandeur are hid. Frequently the trains are shifted during the day, and night, with its blackness, finds the circus cars awaiting their loads in an entirely different section of the town. The drivers are informed of the change, but it is left to their keen perceptions to make the trip by the shortest route. This is no simple accomplishment, in the gloom of streets and with landmarks entirely unfamiliar, but it is performed without blunder or inaccuracy. The number of accidents to man and beast in these nocturnal wanderings is remarkably insignificant, due, in a great measure, to the skill of the reinsmen and their coolness in emergencies. Sometimes steep hills, rough roads, or sharp corners bring disaster, but not frequently. The wagons progress to their destination behind four-, six-, eight-, and ten-horse teams as smoothly, safely, and swiftly as the local doctor goes his rounds.

The money wagon is early off the train and on its way to the lot. Inside is the assistant treasurer of the show, who has been shuffled about continually during the time allotted to slumber, but whom long service has inured to the racking. He is there to guard that part of the coin and bills which has not been expressed to New York. There is not an instance on record of a successful attempt to loot the money wagon of a circus, although many showmen wonder that the apparently inviting opportunity offered has not been seized. This immunity, I suppose, rests on the basis of knowledge that there are no more courageous, determined fighters than circus employees. For daring, hardihood, and bodily prowess they have no superiors. The boldest highwayman may well hesitate before he takes liberties with the money wagon. He would find a man inside ready and experienced in gun play, and a party of circus workmen whose duty it is to be prepared for invaders would appear like men from the ground. If the marauder escaped with his life, much less the plunder he sought, the prediction often made would be inexact.

Arrived at the lot, the money wagon is a scene of stir and activity. The press agent is there to receive the money for newspaper advertising. Then all the bookkeeping which the circus demands in great variety must be accomplished, for the morning is the only period of the day which gives opportunity for the work. Later the sale of tickets and the balancing of accounts engrosses all time and attention. Pay day comes each week to every employee of the circus. The performers are paid on Saturday during the time between the afternoon and evening performances. On Wednesdays, during the afternoon show, the long line of workmen forms and several hours are consumed in the exchange of money. The operation is laborious, for sometimes the coming and leaving of the men is frequent. Each has a name and number for identification assurance, and the two men who make the payments are thoroughly exhausted when the operation is over.

The owner's private car is attached to the last section, a position which makes it certain that the owner be on the scene if there is accident to the other sections. In case of breakdown or other railroad misfortune, his section would speedily overtake and he would thus be soon in personal command. The sections usually halt at the given point within a half hour of one another, and soon the last employee has stumbled over ties and rails toward the lot and all the wagons have departed from the scene. Long lines of empty cars await the repeated activity of night. These cars, incidentally, are as extended as safety and convenience permit, for railroad companies charge for transportation by the single car. The fewer cars drawn from town to town, the smaller the amount of money the circus is called upon to pay.

It is easy to distinguish the performer from his fellow employee as the men leave the cars. The acrobats and gymnasts limp down the car steps as if every bone and muscle were lame and sore, and progress with halting tread toward the lot, very different in aspect from the firm, elastic-stepped men who entered the place the night before. It is an unhappy condition in which every one of the athletes finds himself the morning after the violent exercise of the ring or bar. None of them takes any unusual precaution to guard against physical affliction, and the wonder is that often they are not more seriously handicapped after sleep. After a few preliminary exercises their sound, strong, vigorous constitutions assert themselves and they are ready and eager for any required feat.

The veteran circus man is superficially acquainted with the physical features of most of the towns visited. Alighting from the car, he surveys the landscape and heads straight for the lot. He has been there before and he recalls it all. Here a sleeping car was burned two years ago; in another town two elephants had a thrilling duel to the death; there is the jail where a ticket taker was locked up without just cause; "Mr. Lew" remembers the bank where he secured bonds when a man with a claim for damages attached the ring horses with the mistaken notion that he would be bought off for a large sum of money; through that low bridge a heavy pole wagon once crashed. Every place in the country is associated with some personal incident in the circus man's mind.

I walk often to the lot with a gray-haired man whose form is unbent by age, whose eye is undimmed, and whose active manner still evinces readiness to plan and will to execute. He is one of the ringmasters and has other duties of the arena and the business office. He has dwelt his long life in circus precincts, and for him the whole circus fraternity cherishes a peculiar veneration. Honesty and godliness mark his career, and his is the example pointed out to the circus young. Well may they imitate his virtues and walk in his footsteps! His presence recalls the faint memory of overland journey and one ring, and the stern hardships of the days of long ago. Those were times when his name was familiar wherever the show tent penetrated, and when his exploits made him the marvel of the profession and the prominent feature of performances—for none in all the world could equal his feats of horsemanship and acrobatic skill. From the haunch of the white circus beast he executed revolutions which even the modern show has not duplicated, and aloft he tumbled and turned in dare-devil accomplishments which now only the reassuring stretches of the net concede.

Simple modesty characterized his life of spectacular success, and now, when time has forbidden active participation and a new generation has entered upon the stage, he accepts with cheerful philosophy his relegation, to a uniform which bespeaks only the cracking of a whip. His wife, many years his junior, is one of the conspicuous performers, for he has taught her all the finish and art of bareback riding, and made her one of the cleverest wire-walkers with the show. He is always at her side when she performs, advising, correcting, praising, and, as she elicits admiring gaze, few in the audience recognize his figure as the one in whom so much sentimental interest centres. The press agent, extolling the youth and beauty and grace of the performer, points him out casually to the reporters as her "father" and flatters himself that he is subserving the interests of the show; but if the woman knew of the tale she would promptly put a stop to its circulation. She is proud of her kindly old husband and wants the world to know it. She boasts no circus pedigree, as do most of her comrades, and was schooled in the circus arena after she had reached her majority. She is a living refutation of the tradition that one must be born to the ring.

We watch her rehearsals in the spring with curiosity, and the other performers always profit by the directions and advice the veteran gives her. Sometimes, to his practised mind, she is awkward and slow of comprehension. Then I have seen him jump to his feet and leap to the horse's back. He forgets his forbidding age, in the emotions of the past, and would fain give her the benefit of a demonstration. But his feet have lost their inspiration, his hold is unsteady and his muscles do not respond. He alights rather shamefacedly. The young athletes pat him kindly on the back and cheer him with words of his former glory; and his wife puts her arms around his neck and says he's a dear old fellow. Love and loyalty will be his enduring memorial.

The inherent energy of the circus is never more fully demonstrated than when there is tardiness in arriving at the town of exhibition. The fault is seldom the circus's and generally the railroad's. Connections have been faulty, the engines inadequate to the requirements of the heavy trains, facilities for loading bad, or there has been delay in ferrying the sections. There are no faint hearts or falterers with the show and no weakness in these crises. Out of confusion worse confounded, order and convenience speedily reassert themselves, and the tremendous amount of preparation for the exhibition is rushed to wonderfully quick completion. Sometimes it has been nearly noon before we were able to drag a single wagon from the cars, but the programme for the day has been followed as implicitly as though there had been no hindrances. The parade emerged with customary roar and glare, the performance followed in regular sequence, and left behind was the same satisfactory trail of desolated pockets that the usual early coming would have accomplished.

Sunday is the circus man's day of rest and relaxation. After the pitching of the menagerie and the smaller tents, necessary to the accommodation to the animals, the day is granted for freedom and enjoyment. The start from the Saturday stand is always made the same night, and the Sabbath respite is improved for long railroad runs. The route is so planned in advance that on no one night except Saturday is the journey so long that, everything favorable, there will be tardy arrival. It is not deemed expedient to risk a longer "jump" than eighty or ninety miles unless transportation facilities are unusually advantageous. The trips of one hundred and fifty or two hundred miles are reserved for the night which precedes the day of exemption. So it is that the circus folk, ending their slumber, find the train still on the move, with a possible prospect of several more hours in their cramped quarters. The sagacious ones have examined the railroad schedule the day before and laid in a supply of fruit and food for this contingency. They preconceive how sorely taxed will be the resources of the train restaurant, for circus appetites are voracious in the morning. Chairs are soon placed on platforms and at windows, and the workingmen gather in groups on car tops or under the ample spread of the wagons.

DISEMBARKING FROM THE CIRCUS TRAIN.

These Sunday morning railroad pilgrimages carry the circus through all climates and localities and, unless too protracted, afford a sense of keen enjoyment. There are inviting expanses of woodland and water, moor and mountain. Summer verdure clothes the scenery, and the view is often entrancingly beautiful to the crowd-surfeited vagrants. Smiling villages and beautiful cities pass in procession. The gazing native is bombarded with interrogations as to the proximity of the circus train's ephemeral goal. Sometimes there are brief stops at wayside stations, while the engine takes water or gives place to another iron hauler. Then occurs an exodus from the cars. Men, women and children improve the opportunity to exercise their cramped bodies, for nothing is more distasteful to their active persons than restricted movement, or to invade with hurried dash the humble railroad restaurant. Never before has its composure been so rudely disturbed. Coffee is gulped down eager throats, and the return to the train is made with hands and pockets overflowing with sandwiches. Two sharp warning shrieks from the engine and the start is made anew.

Few of the performers or staff members go to the lot for Sunday meals, although the tent awaits their presence. They register at the local hotels and spend much time in writing and reading. Many take advantage of the chance for a change and spend the night away from their accustomed sleeping apartments. In the evening a large number of the women attend church and the men pass a few hours in simple pleasures. At the lot the scene is one of peace and quiet. The canvas of the "big" and other "tops" which have not been elevated lie passive on the ground ready for the men who will haul them aloft at sunrise. They are not raised until immediate necessity demands, for the reason that the danger of fire or "blow down" is thus minimized in the one and rendered impossible in the other instance. Curious crowds flock about the grounds and are permitted free scrutiny. It is particularly a Sunday assembling-place for women. They desert household cares and domestic duties for the fascinations which invest the circus in repose.

CHAPTER III

EARLY SCENES ON THE LOT

The selection of the place of exhibition is a duty which requires careful study and practical observation and involves a variety of considerations. Ten acres is the smallest piece of ground on which our circus can spread itself, and an unoccupied site of this size which has the requisite advantages is not always easy to find in these days of rapid-growing communities. A plot which had all the conditions demanded the year before may be the foundation of many houses when the show arrives on its next visit. The spot chosen is generally rural in its situation—the claim on space makes this unavoidable—but it imperatively must be urban in convenience. Swift-moving trolley cars have added joy to the circus business, for they make accessible these remote localities. Obviously when transportation facilities are awkward, the show suffers. And so it is that usually we find ourselves settled for the day where stretches of electric wires are a constant menace to towering chariots and a source of terror to their fair occupants. Of course, the conformation of the immediate ground and the condition of the soil are taken into important account in the choice of the lot, but the difficulties which they offer often submit to the mastery of the army of workmen. Water must be convenient, abundant and wholesome.

Sometimes nowhere in a town can be found empty room for all the big and small tents, huddle them as we will. Then the "big," menagerie and side-show "tops" are given places in the allotted limit, and the canvas adjuncts are planted down the road, in neighboring back yards or in distant fields. It is an irritating and inconvenient compromise, but one that cannot be always avoided. These annoying conditions, however, do not present themselves as a general rule. Our destination is more often a fragrant spacious pasture where the air is pure, the sun brilliant and nature's tranquil beauty all-pervading.

The boss canvasman is first on the ground and remains in supreme control of the horde of brawny men who trail after him. With the arrival of the chain-and-stake wagon the active work of erecting the tents begins. The "cook tent" is first placed in position, for food must await the throngs of men, women and children who are on the way. This is a simple and expeditiously accomplished duty, as compared with the elevation of the "big top," a swelling fabric within whose folds fifteen thousand persons can accommodate themselves. The boss canvasman combines with other qualifications a practical knowledge of surveying. His comprehensive scrutiny of the area determines accurately boundaries, positions, extent, lines and angles, and indicates to his experienced mind how best to avoid roughness and depressions and how to overcome the other resistances the tract offers. Sometimes huge rocks or spreading trees make the task one of great difficulty, for it must be accomplished with haste. His examination finished, he unwinds a metal tape line and traverses the lot.

Slender iron rods are planted where he indicates. These are immediately replaced by strong wooden stakes to which the "guys" or ropes of the tents will be fastened. Soon the ground bristles with these pegs, thrust into place with unerring aim and in perfect cadence by gangs of sledge-hammer drivers.

Teams of horses pull the towering centre poles into upright position and the skeleton of the monster is in place. The vast reaches of canvas are unrolled in sections and laced together while flat on the ground. Then the mammoth white cloth rises like a canvas-backed Aladdin's palace and is attached to the side-poles, which are twelve feet high and twelve feet apart around the outer edges of the white spread. The scene is one of bustle and activity. Small boys are pressed into service, receiving a ticket to the show as remuneration. Menagerie, side-show, stable, blacksmith, harness, dressing, wardrobe, and barber tents yield to diligent exertion, and soon the delegated proprietors of the broad green space have finished their morning labors. Meanwhile the wagons and apparatus have arrived, and owner, manager, riders, ringmasters, animal trainers, gymnasts, jugglers, clowns, ticket-sellers and all the rest of the heterogeneous throng put in appearance. Curious crowds rivet their attention upon the unwonted doings. They come from farm and merchandise and from seats of learning and courts of justice, and find keen enjoyment in the sights and sounds.

The "cook tent" is one of the marvels of the modern circus. It was the custom for many years for the circus management to send its employees to the local hotels for their food. The undertaking of providing meals for the army on the grounds was so stupendous that the most comprehensive and well-organized show hesitated to make the essay. Finally, the objections to the old method made the accomplishment imperative. As circuses grew in size, the combined resources of the hotels in many towns were unable to meet the demand made upon them. There was too much delay and unsatisfactory provisions, and the circus felt their injurious effects. The arrangement now in vogue does away with all these difficulties. Advance men see that all the needs of the commissary department are provided for, and meat, vegetables, water and the other requirements await the hand of the chefs. There are two separate and distinct culinary establishments. One is occupied by the workingmen, whose stomachs are not gratified until the tents are raised and all the apparatus is on the lot. This is a wise provision which insures prompt work. There are no laggards in their ranks in the early morning.

Under an adjoining canvas are fed the executive staff and performers, men, women and children. There are three long rows of tables, and crossing them at one end a shorter set of boards where is the owner's place and those of his immediate associates. It is from this position, his abundant family collected around him, that he makes his announcements, administers rebukes and extends praise. He surveys the scene critically and is immensely pleased at the healthy relish which pervades the place. Curious sightseers peer through the apertures and he abruptly bids them retreat with the assurance that "we are not wild animals. We eat just like other human beings." Outside the tent rest hogsheads, from which are dipped panfuls of pure, clear water, for grimy hands and dusty faces. Long towels slung over stretches of rope are ready for use. Scrupulously clean cloths cover the table, and no spot or stain afflicts the dishes. The food, cooked in the open, has its own peculiarly delicious, appetizing flavor. It is served in abundance, and a happier, heartier party never did justice to a meal. Skilful waiters do prompt, experienced attendance. Service and quality could not be improved upon in the large hotels of many cities. As the "cook tents" are the first to be raised, so they are the first to be levelled and packed away on the cars. The last meal of the day is served at five o'clock in the afternoon, and two hours later there is no perceptible trace of the improvised restaurant, save the coals which glow in the twilight.

CIRCUS COOKS PREPARING BREAKFAST.

The harness and blacksmith tents are as complete in their facilities as any stationary establishments. In the former, waxed thread, needle and hammer are busy through the day. The showy equine accoutrements and trappings require constant care, and among the tangled mass of collars, traces, saddles, reins and other framework of straps there is always labor of repair. The blast-furnace of the blacksmith blazes from morning until night, and his anvil knows no rest. There are horses to be shod, iron pieces to be forged, wagons needing attention, and a variety of work which must be done with dispatch and thoroughness.

Across the field in a shady and sheltered spot the ashen cloth of the circus barber shop shows. No detail of a well-equipped city shop is missing. Even is seen the pole, striped red and white spirally, denoting the presence of the profession. Here the men of the circus are shaved and have their beards trimmed and their hair cut and dressed with great expedition and much perfume. It is a time-saving convenience.

The whir of sewing machines is never absent from the wardrobe tent, and seamstresses work with needle and thread from light to dark. Wear and weather work sad havoc with resplendent uniforms and trappings of human and brute, and the need of repair or replenishment is always pressing.

Cages are thrust under the menagerie tent only long enough for the feeding of the animals, and a hasty burnishing of gilt and cleaning of wagon wheel and body. Horses reappear soon, now plumed and ornamented, and drivers don the uniform of the parade. This tent, like its big canvas companion, will be empty and silent, save for the arranging of apparatus, until the parade returns from its formal journey to town.

In the stable tents the Shetland ponies delight the children and command the admiration of the elders. They come from the wild and sterile islands between the Atlantic Ocean and the North Sea, where they run at large. They are very hardy, and their strength is great in proportion to their size. Rough hair covers them, and their manes and forelocks are large and shaggy. Very useful in active, sure-footed work, and very valuable to the show from an artistic standpoint, are these small breeds of horses, but also are they very vicious and tricky. They bite and kick at small or no provocation, at keepers and strangers alike, and frequently engage in violent combat among themselves. They are the subjects of eternal espionage, but human vigilance cannot always thwart their mischief. The dun or tan color, with a black stripe along the back, is prevalent among their shades, and they compose one of the prettiest scenes on the circus lot. The tricks they perform in the ring always meet enthusiastic favor.

In the Southern States, "snack stands" line the limits of the circus lot. Colored people conduct them, and the food they provide is wholesome and wonderful in variety. No Northerner who has not witnessed circus day in the old Confederate section has any adequate conception of the extent to which these eating places flourish. The appetizing odor of food pervades the air, patrons are filled with the exuberance of the occasion, and the scene is one to add a measure to the joy of living. No dish often has a price exceeding five cents, and the ham and chicken and cakes and biscuits served have a peculiar charm of flavor, which sometimes even lures the showman from the canopied canvas of the "cook tent."

Applicants to join the circus come by the score in every town. There are few changes in the ranks, however, during the season, except in the cases of canvasmen and hostlers. These desert, are discharged or find other places frequently. After a spell of rainy weather, never more wearing on man and beast than with the circus, the less stout-hearted or robust leave rapidly for easier work. All the performers contract for the season or longer, and are philosophic and satisfied at all times. Sometimes the eager candidate for circus honors is awaiting us at the railroad station, follows to the lot, and often no rebuff or decided denial of his demand for a position will suffice. This persistent person we turn over to the head clown and watch the cure. He is escorted with great deference to the dressing-room, received by the performers with keen anticipatory delight and ostentatiously welcomed to their ranks. It is explained that he must begin his career as a laugh-provoker. His hair is filled with powdered sawdust, he is daubed with chalk and dye-stuffs, put in tights and ordered to the ring.

There the ringmaster, prepared to do his part, awaits him. The luckless victim feels the sharp lash of the whip on his almost naked legs, and is put through a course of sprouts which finally drives him from the arena, a sorry fun-producing specimen. Desire for sawdust and spangles has left him.

An awkward problem which sometimes presents itself is the replenishing of the horse stables. No stauncher troupe of draft horses can be found anywhere than the circus carries. Great strength is a prime requisite, but they must needs be handsome, handy and gentle. These qualifications are not frequently grouped in one animal. So it is that great care is lavished upon the circus equine that his condition remain all that is necessary. Despite all attention of the practised men of the stables, however, sickness and accidents often send the beasts to the stock farm or the graveyard. Facilities for their treatment in wet weather are inadequate, notwithstanding an expert veterinary always is in attendance upon them, and is on the regular pay roll. The strain of sleeping in a moving train of cars at night and heavy hauling at day is tremendous, and strange, rough roads invite misfortune. Ailing animals cannot be transported, and replacing begins.

At the outset of the season we were in particularly bad straits. A rainy night when we first paraded, in New York, caused an epidemic of pneumonia, which our proficient veterinarian could not stay. The supply of horses diminished rapidly, and in two weeks it was with some difficulty that we accomplished unloading, parade and departure without serious delay. Then were displayed, conspicuously, on the phalanx of stable tents and at the entrance to the lot, announcements that we desired to purchase native animals. The show was then in West Virginia. For a fortnight the scene in the horse quarters resembled a gypsy camp. The owner and his associates knew just what they wanted, made the fact plain and were ready to pay spot cash when they found it. But the farmers and horse traders at once conceived the notion that this was a heaven-sent opportunity to rid their stalls of the aged, infirm beasts which had accumulated on their hands. Concealing defects with adroit craft, they would flourish up to tents and with great gravity of manner dwell upon the merits of the animal which fitted him perfectly for circus requirements. They reckoned not upon the familiar knowledge of the men with whom they dealt. A keen glance or a practised touch revealed all blemishes. No trick or stratagem, and I am sure every one known to sharp equine transactions was employed, availed against the showman's discernment. A favorite dodge was to exhibit the animal in the shadow of the naphtha torches at night, but exposure followed at once. The circus traversed three States before the proper horses were procured.

Meanwhile "Boscow" unremittingly consumes snakes in a gaudy canvas booth at the entrance to the grounds. Clyde, a man of long established integrity and not deficient in lungs, gives personal assurances of the progress of the reptilian feast. "Eighteen years old, not married, pretty; and eats snakes like you eat strawberry shortcake! Eats 'em alive! Bites their heads off!" is his frequently repeated promise, and the constant, eager procession passing his stand and into the ophidian enclosure, testifies to the weight of his forceful eloquence.

Squatting in a cavernous serpentarium, patrons find "Boscow," feminine in appearance only because of long, coarse black hair, surrounded by coiling, crawling reptiles. "She" has presumably just completed an especially elaborate animal meal, for to the nostrils comes the breath of tobacco and upwards winds the suspicion of cigar smoke. But "Boscow" waves away the muttered insinuations which penetrate even into "her" wild, untutored mind, and at the word of command eats ravenously of the amphibian mass which surrounds "her" on all sides.

"Boscow" was captured in the far-off jungles of Africa, Harry, the lecturer explains, and in wonderful words he continues of "her" fight for liberty, the ineffectual efforts to tame "her" savage nature, and "her" sullen refusal to discontinue snake diet. It is very awesome and impressive, and the audience, before making way for the clamoring ones behind, look with renewed interest at the strange creature. "Her" appearance lends belief to the fluent narrative, and to the more shrinking ones is proof of the need of precautionary measures in the dismal clanking of heavy binding chains as "she" springs scowling about the compartment. Little wonder no credence is placed in the bold assertion of one who proclaims that he saw "Boscow's" brother, or surely a near blood relative, perspiring freely as he helped in the erection of the booth that morning. Her kin are, of course, in a remote, uncivilized land, and as ferocious as the girl herself. The incredulous person saunters off with dim wonder at the remarkable likeness filling his mind, Clyde's frantic invitation to go inside pours out tirelessly, and Harry paints again and again the glowing picture of the snake-eating wonder.

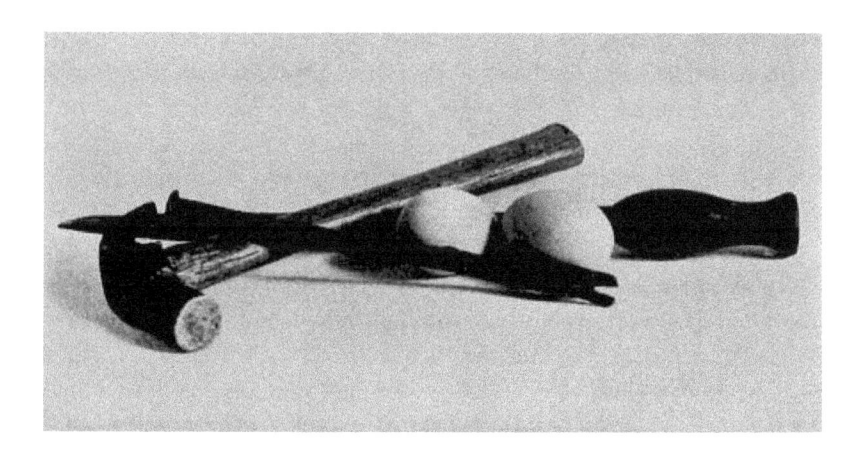

TWO HEN'S EGGS, HAMMER, FILE AND NAIL-CLAW PRESENTED BY A PLEADING, PENNILESS MISSISSIPPI NEGRO BOY TO SECURE ADMISSION. HE GOT IN.

There is nothing like a spell of rainy weather to breed a feeling of despair in the showman. The route has been planned with the idea of evading as far as human foresight permits, unfavorable meteorological conditions, but it is inevitable that sometimes rain and mud and wind be encountered. There can then be nothing more mournful and disheartening than life with the circus. If, for a brief succession of days, performances have to be abandoned, profits are consumed with a ruining rapidity. It is not infrequent that this form of misfortune bankrupts the scantily-financed circus which has started out with hopeful prospects, for the overwhelming expense of maintaining the organization is not reduced whether it remains huddled on the cars or is displaying its glories to lucrative crowds. So resolute and so prepared for exigencies are the bigger shows, however, that nothing less than a flood can prevent unloading and presenting some sort of an exhibition. If the rain is continuous, there is no immediate prospect of relief, and the lot is a quagmire, the animal cages are often left on the cars. A staggering march to the marsh is made by the other vehicles and a semblance of show is given in the menagerie tent. In the space usually allotted to the animals, seats are put in position and a gallant effort made to get some financial return. A doleful, drenching sight it is, horses wallowing in the ring, acrobats and gymnasts shivering and slipping, and clowns feebly trying to call to life the smile of pleasure. Straw is littered over the premises in the endeavor to absorb the moisture, but avails little. Where the stretches of canvas are sewed together the water penetrates through, and muttering spectators leave reluctantly or elevate umbrellas. The heavy laboring of the groaning tent adds to the feeling of misery and melancholy. The circus people gaze longingly across the empty fields where are houses snug and tight. Then the heaped-up gloom of the night, the black, wet journey to the cars and a possible awakening to identical conditions in the morning. These are times that strain the buoyant temperament and the rugged constitution. Sunshine, however, restores human spirits, tarnished gilt and saturated canvas, and drives away the ghastly memory of it all. Exuberance reasserts itself and the panoplied colony emerges in all its former order, convenience and beauty.

It is the first heavy rainfall of the season that brings the most overwhelming woe. The custom of circus owners is to wash their tents with paraffine at the beginning of each season. The waxy mixture renders the cloth waterproof and preserves it from atmospheric influences. The treatment is not efficacious, however, until the fabric has been thoroughly soaked with rain and succeeding sunshine has dried it out. So it is that a dull dread of approaching calamity fills every professional heart when the initial storm sets in. The water falls upon showman and patron as if no so-called protection was above. A wan and spectral "big top" it is at night, sometimes with vivid lightning filling it with sulphur-smelling blazes, and the frail dressing-room tent clinging to it like a luminous bulb.

CHAPTER IV

THE PARADE

Breakfast over, active preparations are on for the parade. Well-fed horses and ponies in shining harness and waving plumes take their places before glittering vehicles; the sound of music is heard from bands perched hazardously high; clowns, charioteers, jockeys, Roman riders join the line; camels and elephants, some bearing a weight of feminine beauty in Oriental costume, make appearance, and a picturesque cavalcade nearly a mile long is in motion.

One of the managers leads the line down to town and back. He has already been over the course once, noting its conditions with caution born of long experience. Sometimes his foresight bids him change the route. A corner is too sharp for the forty-horse team, a hill may be dangerously steep, a bridge too low or unsafe, the road too rough, or perhaps the advance man did not appreciate that at a certain point the parade would "double" on itself.

Behind him a drum corps blows and beats, and then Jeanne d'Arc, in polished armor, with clanking curtains of chain mail. The flush of tan is beginning to tint ears and cheeks under her helmet and her two mounted knights are very happy and proud. She is a young woman who was adopted by a wealthy aunt in Pittsburg, who sent her to Europe to keep her from entering circus life. Her sudden return, romantic marriage with a tattooed man, enlistment as a jockey rider in Cedar Rapids, Ia., and rapid rise to the front ranks of equestriennes is a matter circus folk never tire of discussing.

Through densely crowded streets the procession measures its gaudy passage, a handsome lovelorn young acrobat yearning for the return to the tent, where an eighteen-year-old girl somersault rider eagerly awaits him; the stepmother behind, who doesn't approve of their devotion; a uniformed marshal, whose thoughts are for his wife, seriously ill in a Philadelphia hospital; a brother who fears for his sister; a bicycle rider at the performance, now high on the back of an elephant whose temper has been bad for several days; Sultan, a majestic lion, viewing it all calmly from the top of a high cage; bands playing, horses prancing, wagons rumbling, calliope screaming, clowns frollicking—truly a fantastic panorama. And sometimes ahead, then behind, again on the side, a tramp bicyclist, darting up steps and down, scaling fences, into stores and houses, often one wheel off the ground, seldom on both, but never dismounting.

By the side of the band wagons and behind the shrieking calliope a cloud of boys keeps tireless pace, reeling off mile after mile, but gorged with happiness. Street cars make time with the procession, jammed with passengers and scores hanging to platforms, paying no fares but this eloquent testimony to the passing show. The tigers and lions look bored, and the hyena yawns with accumulated ennui. Behind, the gorgeously caparisoned riders, men and women in tights and spangles and breastplates of shining gold and steel; behind, the richly-decked camels with riders from the great desert and the elephants swaying to and fro with monotonous tread, and near the end of the gaudy line, the fairy outfit of Santa Claus, the old woman of nursery fame, Bluebeard in decapitation attitude and the other tableau wagons of burnished gold and flaming red.

The clowns are very much in evidence. Behind all manner of steeds, from the camel treading like a dusty spectre with his cushioned feet, to the proud pony, and from the four-horse teams to the decrepit agricultural equine; on foot and on elephant and on bicycle; in costume weird and wonderful, they are an amusement-affording part of the cortege. Boys flock by their sides, and their ready wit is equal to all exigencies. Well has the press agent written:

> Clowns on four legs,
> Clowns on two,
> Clowns the cutest you ever knew;
> Clowns on the earth,
> Clowns in the air,
> Clowns in the water,
> Clowns everywhere;
> Clowns in seal-skins,
> Clowns in hair,
> Clowns with whom no others compare;
> Clowns in motley,
> Clowns with wings,
> Clowns that accomplish marvellous things;
> Clowns in dress suits,
> Clowns in kilts,
> Clowns in long skirts,
> Clowns on stilts,
> Clowns that mimic every fad,
> Clowns that make the millions glad,
> Clowns that cause the buttons to fly,
> Clowns at whom you laugh till you cry;
> Clowns of every nation and clime,
> Clowns uproarious all the time,
> Clowns and more than you ever saw,
> Clowns that make the world haw-haw.

The clowns' band is near the end. In grotesque attire, the "musicians" blow and beat on the top of one of the chariots. The production is what the alliterator of the show calls "a slaughter of symphonies, a murder of melodies, a wrecking of waltzes, a massacre of marches, a strangling of songs, a total of terrific tonal tragedies!"

The inevitable hay wagon is in the column, and nimble acrobats toss lightly on its fresh-mown burden. Their costumes are bucolic throughout, but offer no impediment to their agile movements. Country boys look on and marvel. The clown in dilapidated wagon behind tottering horse is not absent. His countryman disguise is so perfect that his identity is not suspected. He narrowly escapes being run down by the big circus wagons; he is always in the way and impeding the smooth progress of the parade; he becomes involved in all sorts of plights, but emerges unscathed. It furnishes great fun for the spectators. Sometimes policemen threaten and oftener take him in custody. Then he tells who he is and the crowd roars again, this time at the bluecoat's expense. Hilarity reigns wherever is his presence.

Above the shrill tones of the fife and the blast of the cornet and the clamor of drums and cymbals, rises the oft-repeated admonition, "Look out for your horses, the elephants are right behind!" A clarion-voiced equestrian rides up and down the line of bespangled magnificence with this warning to those who view the spectacle in wagon or saddle. A quick, keen, trained glance reveals to him the probable effect the "led" animals will have on each equine within eye and scent. He knows, too, what the man who holds the reins is not aware of, that the animal with the hump alarms horses more than his ponderous companion. Often the parade is brought to a standstill while this precautionary person insists that a horse displaying the initial signs of disquiet be removed to a place of safety, or, while with the skill of long practice he assists in subduing a beast whom the distant approach of the procession has already alarmed. Women are his *bête noir*. They have full faith in their horsemanship, they tell him, and, anyway, their horses have been thoroughly trained and broken. Then he is gently but firmly obdurate, accepts with good grace the denunciation to which he is subjected, but sees that the possibility of disaster has been removed before he permits the line to pass. He is a saver of life and limb whose services few but showmen appreciate.

Once the tents are pitched, no weather can be so unpropitious as to thwart the parade. Rain may fall in copious measurement; mud, perhaps, is deep to the knees. But on with the parade! A much weather-beaten and woe-begone lot of performers, to be sure, and a drenched and blinking lot of drivers, but all forgotten when the sunshine comes again. This display is what circus folk call a "wet day" parade. Women and children are excused, much of the finery is kept in the shelter of the tents, men wear mackintoshes and rubber boots, and protecting canvas hides the gilt and glory of the chariots. It has been advertised as "positive," however, and the management must keep faith with the public or lose its confidence. Then, too, it serves to show some of the glory and fame of the organization, whets public curiosity and the possible return of clear skies will draw to the grounds the multitude which, without its promise, would have returned home for the day. Business instinct bids there be a parade without fail.

Down in the town the press agent is paying the newspaper bills for advertising, distributing tickets, and seeing to it that editors and reporters are put in good humor, and arranging as far as it is in his power that notices before and after the performances are complimentary. Sometimes he accompanies a body of reporters to an advantageous position and they survey the parade together. He buys cigars and refreshment—at the circus's expense—and impresses his companions as being affable, courteous and a good fellow generally. They part company on fine terms of friendship, and he assures them that he will consider it a personal affront if they don't all come to the show and bring their friends. Sometimes his hospitality has been so affecting that they will be tempted to write pretty things about him; that the "genial press agent" is with the circus, or, "the circus is fortunate to have so efficient an employee" and, following a description of his virtues. But his prudence begs them to desist, for he knows "the boss" doesn't approve. The owner takes the view that newspaper space devoted to the circus itself is more to pecuniary advantage than an enumeration of the qualities of the press agent.

The keen eye of the general manager follows the parade on its tortuous journey. If there be accident or delay, or any other unforeseen trouble, he is at the scene promptly and takes command. A two-seated carriage follows the line. In it he, the press agent, and the circus detective are conveyed back to the lot. It is a convenience which dispenses with a hot, dusty walk or an uncomfortable journey in packed trolley cars.

The "$10,000 Beauty" was a parade feature of one of the big circuses for several years. The owner, a man deep in many schemes for advertising his tented organization, boldly asserted that he paid that amount of salary to a young woman who proceeded through the streets striving to live up to her reputation for grace and charm, on the back of one of the largest elephants. She wore a pained and anxious look as she clutched grimly to the animal's canopied hide, and there was little appeal to aesthetic nature. Later she exhibited her harmonious proportions in the menagerie tent. She is now embellishing the variety stage, whence she emerged upon the circus world, and where, perhaps, her costly beauty is better appreciated.

Many will remember the telescopic affair which P. T. Barnum exhibited in his parades for several seasons in the early '70's. It was a massively carved chariot, and he called it the "Temple of Juno." When extended to its full height, by means of internal machinery, it reached an altitude of forty feet. A gorgeous effect was given it by the precious metals which studded it and by numerous mirrors. Upon an elevated seat, just beneath a rich and unique oriental canopy of the most elaborate finish, sat, in perfect nonchalance, the representative queen, surrounded by gods and goddesses in mythical costume. Elephants, camels and dromedaries completed the tableau. During that period of his career, a season of great prosperity, Mr. Barnum used frequently to lecture on temperance in his tents. He was shrewd enough to appreciate how much to his pecuniary advantage was his devotion to what he called the "noble cause." Crowds came as much to get a glimpse at him and to hear him talk as for a sight at the circus.

CHAPTER V

THE SIDE-SHOW

Order has come out of the confusion at the lot when the parade returns. All is in readiness for the performances, seats and stands and rings and trapezes in place, and every man at his post. The cages are dragged from the parade to the menagerie tent, the horses led to their canvas stables, and elephants push the red and gilt vehicles into place. Down drops the sidewall, ropes are set, and the preparation is complete.

Stolid yokels fill the enclosure in front. Two men are proclaiming with fluency and skill and oratorical effect the wonders of the side-show, and a row of huge banners adds weight to their discourse. Pictured by word and brush are the wild man, the midget, the Egyptian giant, the woman ventriloquist, the knife throwers, the fortune tellers, the electric lady, the snake charmer, the others who make up the collection of oddities, and the group of negro jubilee singers. The band thumps seductively inside and frequently, as an evidence of good faith, one of the freaks is called to the front for a moment's survey. Doubts vanish and the crowd hesitates no longer, when suddenly as the *pièce de resistance* is brandished aloft, impaled on a slender iron rod, a raw hunk of beef. It is to be the wild man's dinner!

By far the most interesting specimen in our side-show is this wild man. His history is long and eventful. The side-show lecturer tells it vividly, many times a day, and invariably the same when he is not in a facetious mood. The narrative, however, is always thrilling, never commonplace. A curtain shrouds the interior of the cage in which the creature "lives and subsists in a state of nature." Pulled aside, it reveals a gloomy den, half filled with hay, where crouches, clawed and tusked, and scantily clad in skins, the rude savage. The fleeting and obscure view of the monster afforded is amply satisfying to the timid, and the venturesome see the curtain drawn, impressed. A discharged employee in a spirit of malice spread a tale of unexpected exposures. The fellow asserted that once the wild man was eagerly "shooting craps" with a colored canvasman, and a second time had hastily torn a clay pipe from his mouth and become again a weird, uncivilized being. The manager was very indignant over the infamous recital; and that very evening came a full exoneration. The wild man escaped. (Business had been unsatisfactory for several days.)

The alarm was sounded throughout the town and spread terror. We all said we feared the worst. Armed men were sent in pursuit. The fugitive was captured in a forest back of the lot and returned, shrieking, biting and fighting fiercely, to his den. Order was restored and the circus turned away a thousand persons for lack of room at the evening's performance. The side-show was not empty of visitors for a month afterwards.

We retain the services of our wild man with some difficulty. His wife, a very indiscreet colored woman from Vermont, has a pernicious habit of appearing inopportunely and accusing our black prize of gambling away his wages and not providing for the support of his family. She is ample of form, emphatic in manner, and prodigal of words, and when she begins to bellow and boister, side-show proceedings stop abruptly and the overwhelmed orator hangs his diminished head and yields verbal supremacy. It is not until she receives from the management positive assurance of a cash advance that she can be persuaded to retreat. At these times the wild man is a very meek and subdued person, and no amount of urging will lure him from the security of his cage until his wife is well out of town.

The original circus wild man, the denizen of Borneo, was white, but his successors have almost invariably had dark skins. "Waino" and "Plutano," exhibited together, are now before the public. "Tom" and "Hattie," wild children from Australia, are dead. "Wild Rose" and "Wild Minnie" are still in the field of savage honor, as is "Old Zip, the What-is-it?" whose head is cone-shaped, and who utters mournful guttural sounds.

The life of the professional wild man is an unhappy one at best. The story is told of a Baltimore, Md., colored man, who, finding himself penniless in Berlin, Germany, enlisted as an untamed arrival from Africa with a small American circus then playing abroad. He endured the torture he was compelled to undergo for a month and then stole away to a hospital. He was required to explain how and why he came there.

"You see, boss," he observed sadly, "I'se been working here, got ten dollars a week to play wild man. I was all stripped 'cept around the middle and wore a claw necklace; had to make out as if I couldn't talk. 'Twas mighty tiresome to howl and grin all day. Then times got hard. I had to eat raw meat and drink blood. The circus man, he stood off as if he was afraid of me and chucked meat on the floor to me. I had to lean over, pick it up in my teeth and worry it like I was a dog. It was horse meat and pretty tough, boss, but it brought crowds for a while. Then it got dreffful cold for a nigger with no clothes on and they put a snake around my neck. I couldn't stand that, so I'se come to the hospital."

He was given clothes and medical treatment, which he sorely needed, and a kindly American sent him back to Maryland.

Calvin Bird, a negro who hailed from Pearson, Ga., was a famous wild man for several years with divers small circuses, and toured most of the country, mystifying all who saw him and sending them away impressed with a conviction that he was all he was represented to be. Not until he appeared at a Syracuse hospital with a request that his horns be removed was the secret of his unnatural appearance disclosed. Under his scalp was found inserted a silver plate, in which stood two standards. Into these, when he was on exhibition, Bird screwed two goat horns. Thousands of people had paid admission to see the curved bone projections and hear him bark. The artificial additions were the idea of a physician in Central America who gave the man an anaesthetic and inserted the plate. The operation of removing the support was a simple one and Bird started for home from Syracuse with a normal head a few days later. The wild man business had got monotonous, he said, and anyway, he had made enough money out of his deception to maintain him in idleness for a long time.

The "electric lady" is one of the phenomena of our side-show, and a source of great wonder to the gullible visitor. She is saturated with the mysterious force. A continuous supply passes from her finger tips to whoever touches her flesh. Scoffers are confounded at the manifestation, and there is a general feeling among the side-show sightseers that she is a supernatural being. There is nothing indicating a violation of natural law in the lady's appearance, and nobody appears to enjoy the curiosity she excites more than her own merry self. A strange feature of the exercise of the invisible agent is that it generates only for commercial purposes. For instance, the power leaves her when the performance closes for the night, and does not develop again until she is on exhibition the following day. Then, too, the current confines itself to a fixed spot. It passes away instantaneously if she moves from her chair.

The "electric lady" in private life is a very domestic and studious person. She is Mrs. E. N. Willis, whose husband is one of the managers of the tent and a recognized authority on "freaks." When I asked her for a contribution to the story of the side-show she took pencil and paper and evolved the following product. It was done under the circus canvas on a hot September afternoon in Illinois, while country visitors stared in wonder at the sight of the "freak" in the act of composition and thought. It is attached in the exact phraseology in which it was handed to me.

"So much has been written regarding circus life as seen only in the 'Big Show,' it will not come amiss to chat a while with a member of the side-show fraternity. When the parade returns to the show grounds, it is followed by a large crowd of people, who have been invited by men with megaphone voices to witness a series of free exhibitions which are used as a means of getting the people together for the opening of the side-show, which is the attraction until the 'Big Show' is ready to admit its visitors at one p.m. The side-show presents a most attractive appearance to the rural visitor, showing as it does upon huge banners the many wonderful sights to be seen within.

"As a means of collecting the followers, a platform is erected directly in front of the side-show entrance. In showmen's parlance it is known as a 'bally-hoo stage,' where, as promised the multitude, these free exhibitions are given.

"Fearing that there may be a few stragglers or sweethearts who have failed to keep up with the procession, and wishing to give them all an equal chance, the band is called outside, and with great strength plays its loudest and swiftest selections. Then the principal orator mounts the 'bally-hoo stage,' and striking upon a huge triangle enjoins silence. In glowing terms he describes the row of paintings, proving the truthfulness of his assertions by bringing out a few of the subjects and dilating upon their merits. After this there is another 'hurry up' tune, and then pandemonium reigns supreme, as from their elevated stands the ticket-sellers, each trying to outdo the other in lustiness of tone, proclaim the price of admission—ten cents. Very few resist the eloquence of the orator and the cries of the ticket-sellers, and in a short space of time the outside workers have a chance to rest their lungs, as nearly all have passed inside.

"In the old days of circus business the side-show was justly styled the annex or museum department, and contained only living curios and a performance of Punch and Judy. Of late years this has been greatly changed, there being such a scarcity of freaks of nature that vaudeville acts, and even minstrel shows, have been introduced to fill up this vacuum. The interior is in charge of a lecturer, who is usually either a magician or a Punch and Judy man, he thereby serving a double purpose.

"There is always a feature upon which the side-show revolves, either a giant or some other wonderful freak of nature, and it always occupies a high platform in the centre of the canvas. The other stages are arranged in horseshoe shape, and upon these the different curios are seated. All side-shows have a snake enchantress, this being an attraction that never fails to please, and the rural visitor stands open-mouthed, with a look of astonishment as the lady lifts these large serpents one by one from their boxes and allows them to coil about her person. She is supposed to answer all questions put to her regarding the reptiles, and is asked many strange ones, such as 'Do you keep them on ice?' 'How do you feed them?' 'Are they stuffed?' 'Did you catch them yourself?' As experience has made her quick-witted, she is ever ready with a reply. The other curios are generally a midget, a long-haired lady, or a tattooed man.

"Few would be considered complete without a mind reader or fortune teller, who by merely tracing the lines of the hand is able to foretell the future. So, when Mary and John stand before her, the lines of Mary's hand always read that John is the favored suitor and is to be her husband, while those in John's hand plainly indicate that Mary is for him alone, and that their union will be blessed with many little ones; which good news sends them giggling and blushing on their way, thoroughly satisfied at having parted with their money, as it has brought them such good results. All curios have the privilege of selling their photos, which is really a part of their revenue, and many a stray dime is coaxed from the pockets of the country visitor to that of the curio who is collecting a 'pork chop fund' for the winter. The initiated photo-seller knows which States will be the most productive. This calls to mind a remark made by a giant while on a trip through Canada. One day after a fruitless endeavor to foist his photos on the public, he demanded:

"'How long here? Me want to go back to Yankee-land.'

"Thus he proved that the Yankees part with their dimes more readily than the Canucks.

"In order to fill the side-show with small circuses there is always a candy stand, and whenever there is a lull in the proceedings the voice of the candy 'butcher' may be heard calling his wares in this manner: 'Strawberry lemonade, ice cold, is five cents to-day. Lemonade, peanuts, cakes, candies, everything is five cents.'

"The space not taken up by stages is usually occupied by slot machines, and many a stray nickel is dropped into them during the day. The lecturer, after going the rounds and giving a detailed description of each curio, concludes the performance with Punch and Judy, which, though the oldest attraction before the public, is always a source of amusement for the little folks, and even the grown folks laugh and cheer as if they had never seen it before. This being finished, the reed manipulator steps from behind the frame and explains to the gaping multitude how easily any one can do the same with the aid of a reed made by himself of silver and silk and 'only costing ten cents.' Children and grown folks alike, in their eagerness to obtain one, push and almost knock one another down, and within a few seconds old and young alike have them in their mouths trying to say 'Oh! Judy, go get the baby.' The side-show has been likened to a church fair, there being something doing every time one turns around.

BAREBACK RIDERS READY FOR THE RING.

"The band is always placed upon a high platform directly behind the entrance, so that only a thin canvas separates it from the outside public. This is done in order that its noise may be easily heard by the passing visitors, whom the ticket sellers are always trying to entice to part with their dimes to see the many wonders exhibited within. This band stage is also used for the minstrel and vaudeville performances which are given as frequently as the occasion demands. The side-show may be justly termed a continuous performance, as there is always something going on to entertain the visitors, who are continually dropping in. When the eloquence of the orators fails to arouse the many hangers-on who have become listless, a curiosity is occasionally brought out upon the 'bally-hoo stage,' and the huge triangle is struck upon to stir up those who are still wavering. There is no let-up until all the people have left the big show and concert. There is then an opportunity for these hard-worked people to eat supper and get a rest until 6:30, when the side-show is again opened and remains in operation until the big show is over, about ten p.m."

Hassan Ali, the Egyptian giant, eight feet two inches tall (one has the orator's word for it), comes each year from the land of his nativity to arouse American wonder and earn American money. He is the pest of hotel keepers on the route, for on Sunday nights he chooses to pass the time for slumber away from the cramped recesses of the circus car and in the regulation bedstead of commerce. The view of Hassan, dreaming of his far-off home, with his brown legs protruding, from the knees down, over the foot-board and his skull rammed against the headpiece, is a sight people flock from all parts of the house to witness. About midnight, generally, there is a noise like an explosion, a rattle, crash and shimmer. The other circus guests turn over and resume sleep; they know the familiar sound, it is the shattering of the giant's bed. The landlord, hurrying to the apartment, finds Hassan on the floor, enveloped in slats, sheets, counterpane and mattress. This is almost a weekly performance and causes Hassan to breathe awful Egyptian imprecations against modern American furniture. No visitor to the side-show has ever approached him in height, and only one person, an aged man wearing a G. A. R. badge, has been able to seize, by standing on a chair, the photograph guaranteeing circus admission which the giant holding between upraised fingers and resting on the floor is accustomed to offer as a reward for the feat. Hassan was much mortified over the veteran's accomplishment, but finds balm in the consciousness that no one else has duplicated the achievement. His favorite exploit is to spread his extended fingers from edge to edge of the top of an ordinary waterpail. If you think it a simple digital trick, try it.

The whole energies of a slender man with a trim figure are devoted to entertaining the side-show visitors. He talks almost unceasingly from morning until night in brief but lucid descriptions of the assembly of oddities. His addresses are delivered with great ostentation and search after effect. He is a man of easy wit and repartee, and of tact and practical intelligence; qualifications necessary to the successful conduct of his vocal calling. Each "freak," barring the "wild man," has for sale personal photographs, the receipts for which the management lays no claim to. This is an important part of their incomes, and the lecturer's failure to call attention to the offering brings upon him reproach and censure. I attach one of his harangues, exactly as he delivered it one afternoon before an audience of grinning Connecticut countrymen. It is interesting as a truthful reproduction of a style of unique oratory which prevails nowhere else.

"Now in about five minutes we will start our regular show in here and have it all over forty-five minutes before the circus commences. (The band blows hard for five minutes.) Everybody pay your attention this way. We commence our show here first. I call your attention to Signor Arcaris and sister. They will entertain you with a wonderful performance known as the impalement act, better known as knife-throwing, without a doubt the best act of its kind in the world. (The act and music.) Now down this way next. I take great pleasure in introducing Princess Ani, the wonder worker and mind reader. We will have what is known as spirit calculations on the blackboard. We will have a number of gentlemen place some figures on the board. The minute you place a figure on the board she knows what figure you place there, although she is blindfolded. She can describe anything and tell you while blindfolded what you are thinking about.

"Now, ladies and gentlemen, I am going to tell you how this lady tells fortunes. She reads the lines of your hand. Every line denotes some peculiar trait in your character. Tells you what you ought to do for your own benefit; tells you what talent you possess; tells you when you are going to get married; tells you how many children you are going to have, if any. The line is there in your own hand, you can't get away from it. Tells your lucky day, lucky number, family affairs, love affairs. Tells how long you ought to live by the life line of your hand! Now, it is all private. She don't tell it out loud. First she explains about the large lines. She whispers so that no one can hear but yourself. And for the small lines you get what is known as the number. The rest your hand-reading calls for is all printed on this slip of paper. No two alike. Every one's fortune is different. Just show her your left hand. The price fifteen cents all the way through. Walk right up and show her your left hand.

"Now to the stage. I call your attention to the smallest lady ever placed on exhibition, Miss Bertha Carnihan, twenty-nine years of age, stands thirty-nine inches in height and weighs thirty-eight pounds. The most perfectly formed little lady on exhibition. She is well educated; has been all over the world. Step up and have a talk with her. She will answer all questions in regard to herself. She also has her photographs for sale.

"Now direct your attention to the large stage in the centre. You will be entertained by Professor Lowry's Nashville students. (When the negro concert is finished, the "big song book, words and music, fifty songs, five cents a copy," are sold.) Now, fix your interest this way, please. I call your attention to Miss Millie Taylor, better known as the Queen of Long-haired Ladies. This lady has without a doubt the longest hair of any lady before the public. The length of the lady's hair is seven feet four inches. Step up and examine it for yourselves. She also has her photos. Now we come to Miss Julien, the world's greatest snake hypnotist. The lady will entertain you with her large den of living monster reptiles, introducing anacondas, boa constrictors, pythons and the turtle-head snake of Florida. (The performer coils snake after snake around her form.) The lady now has one hundred and sixty-eight pounds of snake around her body, neck and arms. You will find her entertaining to converse with. She will tell you all about snakes, etc. She also has her photographs for sale.

"Over this way next. I call your attention to the crowning feature of our sideshow. The tallest man in human history, Hassan Ali, better known as the Egyptian giant. Born in Cairo, Egypt, twenty-six years of age, stands eight feet two inches in height and weighs three hundred and twelve pounds. To give you a better idea in regard to his height and reach we will allow the tallest man in the audience to stand on this high chair. The giant will stand on the ground. If the man reaches up and touches the photograph Hassan Ali holds up between his fingers, we will make him a present of a ticket, taking him all the way through the big show. There (pointing) is a tall man. Would you be kind enough to stand on this chair and reach with him. All right, you see (turning to the audience) he comes about six inches from it. This gives you an idea in regard to the size of the giant's hand. Here is a good-sized water pail. See how far you can span it Goes about half way. The giant spans it. His fingers go two inches over the rim. Now, he has no thick soles on his shoes, no high heels. There's his foot, No. 18. He also has his photographs for sale.

"Now pay your attention over that way. That's Neola, the electric lady. By shaking hands with her, you will receive a slight current of electricity, the same as you would from a battery. Don't be backward, walk right up and shake hands with her. She won't harm you. She also has photos.

"Now, the wild man! Down this way for the wild man! Now, stop that crowding there! Take your time, remember there are ladies and children in the crowd. (He pulls the curtain aside and pokes at the inmate with an iron bar.) There he is, with flat head and low forehead, showing he has very little brain. You notice the maniac look of the eyes, just the same as a beast. He has teeth just like a lion, arms four inches longer than our arms and walks on all fours. Captured in the everglades of Florida, a little over four and a half years ago. Handcuffed and shackled ever since he was caught. Now if you stop to think, you know there is a cause for a monstrosity of that kind. Just before he was born his mother was frightened by a beast. It left the mark on that freak of nature, just as you see for yourselves. Half Indian, half negro, don't understand a word, don't talk, growls like a beast, eats nothing but raw meat. (He draws the curtain.)

"Now pay your attention there. You will be entertained by musical Swarts. (A man gets melody from bells and various instruments.) Over this way next. The old-time funny Punch and Judy. (He enters a booth, gives the familiar show and reappears.) Now, I will show you how I change my voice. It is done with a reed, made of silver and silk. All you have to do is place it on your tongue and talk right. The sound of the words goes through the reed just like this. (He illustrates.) That's the way to do it. There are full directions how to use it. Ten cents, three for a quarter. If they don't blow as I represent, hand them back and I will give you back your money. (When the sales are finished he concludes in loud tones:) The big show commences in five minutes. All over in here."

The lusty-lunged orators on the outside make a great clamor as the crowd passes out, and one of them shouts: "The gentlemanly lecturer will now pass around again, explaining the curiosities, monstrosities and freaks of nature. Come on! Come on!" The heartless band lures with brazen notes and the scene is repeated without variation.

No feature of the side-show is more keenly relished in the country towns than the Punch and Judy show. The lecturer works the figures and carries on the dialogue. The movements of the puppets are managed simply by putting the hands under the dress, making the second finger and thumb serve for the arms, while the forefinger works the head. Punch's high back, distorted breast and long nose give an increased zest to his witticisms, and his career of violent crime is followed with absorbed attention until he is dragged away to expiate it, and the curtain falls amid the shouts of his conqueror.

The freak business is divided into about three varieties, foreign, domestic and fake. In the first class, the collectors travel all over the world in search of rarities, but the very best freaks come from India and the Malay peninsula. In those countries there are people who breed freaks. They buy young children and animals and deform them while their bones are soft, by all manner of means. Then they are constantly on the lookout for genuine, natural freaks, and in those lands the birth of a freak occurs very frequently. The headquarters of this business is at Singapore. There are, too, a number of men who devote themselves to the discovering and placing of freaks of all kinds and varieties, and scarcely a day goes by in winter that we do not receive photographs and illustrated circulars from some freak merchant or other. Of course, there are faked freak men—a perfect host in themselves. If the proprietor of some little show needs an additional attraction and does not have any money to hire something good—for, like everything else, freaks have their price—he can get something for little money that will serve his purpose. The real, genuine, live freaks always command high prices—from $50 to $800 per week each—and travel all over the world in order to exhibit themselves.

CHAPTER VI

AT THE MAIN ENTRANCE

I have always regarded the two men who sell tickets with a feeling of profound awe and solemn wonder. There is something almost uncanny about their daily exhibition. Their flying hands put to shame the clutching display of the octopus. No quicker-brained, more resolute or more peculiarly gifted men are with the show. They face, undaunted and calm, twice a day, a scene of confusion, disorder and clamoring demand which would put to his heels one not fitted perfectly by nature and experience for the part. To see them working their hands with lightning rapidity, directing, advising and correcting, is to me as interesting a study as the whole passing show affords.

When the crowd begins to gather about the ticket wagon ready with the price of admission, it would make infinitely easier the work of the men inside if the sale began then. But business astuteness bids delay. The throng grows fast, fills the enclosure and swarms over the grounds. The side-show orator, meanwhile, directs his seductive eloquence at the perspiring mass and reaps a harvest. This is an advantage gained by no undue haste in distributing tickets.

While this preliminary maneuvring is very gratifying in its results to the management, the burden it accumulates upon the two anxious men in the ticket wagon grows every minute. When finally the signal to begin operations is given, they face a sea of upturned, distorted, perspiring faces, and aloft the air is peppered with hands brandishing admission money. Everybody is irrational, unreasonable and excited. Children cry, women are on the verge of collapse, and men push and strain and mutter strange oaths. Uniformed employees strive in vain to maintain order. The wheels of the red wagon have been buried to the hubs, or it would be swept away in the rush. The mad, violent struggle continues for an hour, and thousands force their path or are carried bodily to the window and labor away with the cherished strips of printed pasteboard. A mountain of bills and coin grows and is toppled into baskets at their side. Soon these are filled and money litters the floor. There is no chance to assort or collect it now. With eyes fixed steadily before them, fingers and hands never lingering or sluggish, but intercepting a counterfeit offering like a flash, they work as if human automatons. Not until solitary arrivals denote the end of the rush do they relax. Thousands of dollars have changed hands in the brief period, yet the scene will be duplicated a few hours hence and the day will record a balance as correct in detail as the most exacting banking institution's.

There is a popular misapprehension about the moral purposes of the men in the ticket wagon. The impression seems to prevail among many sensible persons that they are modern highwaymen, lurking there for prey. An intimate knowledge of their character and conduct makes a definite denial only fair to them. In the swift shuffle of money, there is no intention on their part to take advantage of the circus's patron. It is the fixed design of the management to inspire a feeling of security and confidence, and the selection of ticket-sellers has this end in view. Dismissal and possible criminal prosecution would be the penalty of detected "short change" or other swindling methods.

There is only one legitimate source of outside profit, and that is furnished by the "walkaway," circus vernacular for the person who unconsciously leaves his change behind. He is legion, strangely enough, and more remarkable still, it seldom seems to occur to him to return for his own. When he does it is promptly given him. Ticket-sellers insist vehemently that the "walkaway's" contribution is not more than enough to reimburse them for mistakes in count which are unavoidable in the tumult, and more frequently than not to the benefit of the purchaser. Whether their comrades accept this assertion without reservation is not a subject to be discussed here.

Rates of admission are conspicuous everywhere. Children under two and a half years of age are admitted free; from that age to ten a half-ticket is required, and older persons must pay full charge. Wonderful and varied are the devices resorted to in the effort to evade legitimate payment. Children who at home are in their teens have dwarfed to babyhood at the circus entrance. Parents glibly insist that robust offsprings are under nine years, and panting fathers and mothers present themselves, in the palpable attempt to deceive, with an armful of boy or girl who has reached the full-rate limit. Watchful and inexorable door-keepers receive them, demand and finally are handed the correct sum, and composedly hear themselves styled "a pack of villains and swindlers." Ill-grace characterizes those who would cheat the circus.

To the main entrance come the hundreds of written orders for tickets, issued by the advance agents who have covered the district with bills and posters. As a precautionary measure against imposition, two sets of keen-eyed employees have subsequently prowled over the routes and made note when storekeeper or householder has not kept faith. If the flaring advertisement has been removed, disfigured, or hidden under that of a rival show, a memorandum is made. Thus a list of those who are and who are not entitled to recognition is in the hands of the management when the doors open. Each claim presented to the ticket taker has a corresponding number on the large sheet of paper which the general manager holds, and whether or not the holder enters free depends on its report. Very crestfallen and embarrassed, generally, is the man who thought he could profit without rendering service in return. He had not calculated on the thorough business system with which he was in contact. If the applicant has kept his promise he is welcomed to the show, given what his order calls for in the way of seats and number of admissions, and passes inside.

Each one of the men at the main entrance understands his manifold duties perfectly and there is no confusion. Annoying problems enough present themselves, but the quick-witted, ready circus man solves them without hesitation. Complaints innumerable flow to the main entrance, but everybody receives a fair hearing and just treatment in so far as human effort can bring it about. Fault-finding women are the bane. There is almost no extreme of compromise to which the showman will not go to rid himself of the presence of a member of the other sex when she is wrought up over a conviction that she has been imposed upon. She blocks the passage way, gesticulating madly, protesting volubly and threatening all manner of things. She is generally tall and angular, wears spectacles, carries a cotton umbrella, has a crying child by the hand and is famous in the town as a virago. Dutch and Curley cower before her outburst, and the general manager promises her all she demands if she will only pass on. With a parting volley of abuse she flaunts into the menagerie tent and a feeling of great relief pervades all. Her reappearance, with a lament about the unsatisfactory locality of her seat, may be confidently expected later.

BEFORE THE CROWD COMES.

Vigilant canvasmen picket the stretches of cloth, alert lest the small boy or his older relative crawl under the fabric and gain free admission. The duty is one demanding keen eye and active body, for once the canvas folds after the invader he is generally secure from capture; a scamper under the low rows of seats or into the crowd eludes successful pursuit and recognition. So watchful, however, are these patrolmen and so obdurate against pleading juvenile persuasion that surreptitious entrance is effectually barred. The circus-fascinated but impecunious youngster must needs vicariously satisfy his longing by turning handsprings outside the barrier. The stirring band music carried to his ears conjures immeasurable pleasures in his mind and is madly irritating.

The press agent receives his newspaper guests at the main entrance. They have been provided with tickets bearing his name. To the reporter assigned to write up the circus and to the responsible heads of the newspaper he gives slips of paper passing them into an enclosure from which is afforded an undisturbed survey of all that is transpiring, and brings to closer view the excelling features of the performance. Later he joins them there, explains the show's superiority over all competitors and is generally entertaining. He presses peanuts and lemonade upon them and sends them away in friendly mood.

That manly young fellow who appeared from the inner recesses of the festive tent for a whispered conversation at the main entrance with the general manager is Fred Ledgett, equestrian. He is one of the principals in the season's romance of the circus. Dallie Julian, eighteen years old, who turns back somersaults from the broad, rosined haunch of her horse Gypsy, is the other party to the charming affair. What they dared and suffered before they could win the countenance and support of management and relative and carry out their matrimonial longing, only those who know intimately the prosaic circus institute can appreciate. If there is one thing frowned upon more than all others in tented life, it is adventures of the heart. But Fred and Dallie emerged triumphant and conquering, and the seed of love sown in April came to golden harvest in Iowa, many miles transplanted, where an earnest, curious company of show people witnessed the wedding ceremony and participated in the celebration.

My mind reverts to the early spring when little Dallie, done up in a heavy coat and sitting on one of the tubs which served as a seat for a trick elephant, was holding an informal reception in Madison Square Garden. Preparations for the opening of the circus were in full swing—literally in some instances—for the acrobats, practising for the first time in a new place, were suspended by "mecaniques"—the leather belts with rope attachments that made living pendulums of them when they missed their try. Even one of the bareback riders, forming a pyramid on her husband's shoulders, while he went around the ring on three horses, had the life-saving apparatus around her waist. For she was new at the business and her husband was not letting her take any more chances than he could help. And while father and mother were doing their great aerial act on horseback, both of them looking as though only boy and girl, their two-year-old baby cooed down at the ringside, brought over from Boston to spend three weeks with them. She thought it was fine when her mother jumped and balanced, but her mother thought of nothing except not to fall off and not to hang her husband with the rope that was her safeguard. They were in the middle ring and beside it, swathed in top coats and wrappings of all kinds, were performers waiting for their turns to go in. From beneath their street clothes came glimpses of pink and white fleshings with slippers to match, and over the slippers were clogs, wooden-soled shoes, with leather tops, to prevent their feet from being injured while walking in the ring.

The circus was getting ready to open and everybody was practising to start in a blaze of glory. In one of the end rings a woman was riding bareback, "the best hurdle jumper in the business" said one of the men. It looks easy to run and jump on a horse, but it requires work and practice. Not being a dress rehearsal, every one was in working togs, and the women were wearing bloomer suits, with waists of red, pink and blue, and with that innate sense of decoration that is part of the true artist in the ring, each wore a rosette in her hair that matched the suit.

Dallie's interest was centred on the ring where her aunt, who is also her foster mother, was breaking in a new horse.

"Many of the people use the company's horses, but my aunt has her own and so have I," she explained. "She always breaks them herself and this one is new to the business; that is why there is a rope on him and the ringmaster hangs to it. You see the horse might get frightened and bolt over the side or try to go through the doorway," pointing to a niche that served as an entrance; "there is a man standing at the door to prevent the horse from going out."

The horse was perfectly well aware of the fact and not altogether reconciled, although he was fast approaching that state. Ropes swinging from all sorts of corners where trapezes and "looping-the-loop" contrivances were being put up disconcerted him, but the rope and whip were arguments that appealed in inducing him to stay.

"He will be all right before the performance," Dallie went on with the air of a connoisseur. "There will be two more rehearsals to-day and some chance to practise to-morrow. I am riding the same horse I ride always," she went on, tucking her small feet out of the way of dirt and draught, "and it is lucky for me because I have only been practising two weeks this season. You see I was in the hospital last winter, and all I got of the circus was hearing the band play as I lay in bed while all the others were getting ready for this season. But I practised a lot this year and now I do better than I did last year."

In the upper ring the Rough Riders were putting their horses through their acts and the horses were not altogether pleased. The thing they hated most was being made to lie down when they did not feel the least bit tired, and many of them were inclined to argue the matter until the whip convinced them that really they preferred to do what was wanted. The whip as a convincer in a circus is a great ethical force. At one end of the course were the acrobats doing a complete double shoulder twist. They were swinging by ropes attached to their belts when they missed a leap.

"You see," said Dallie, shedding the great white light of information, "they have never done their turn here before and they are used to a smaller place, so they are practising to get distances. If one of them should miss and fall it would hurt, for they haven't any net under, but the 'mecanique' will keep them swinging clear from the ground. You ought to see the 'mecanique' in the rings of the winter quarters. They are put on people just learning to go bareback. Sometimes they miss a horse and the persons go swinging round and round the ring until they land on their horses again. It is awfully funny. Some of the people are scared this season because they are new and there are a lot of new horses and so they are nervous. My aunt told me the other day she could not sleep nights for worrying about me and how I would get through, but I told her she was silly. I will get through all right and there is no use any way in worrying, even if anything does happen."

"And isn't it remarkable that some persons do not get hurt?" she went on. "Now, here are all of us and there hasn't a thing gone wrong to hurt any one. Why, yesterday one of the walking tight wires broke when there were five people on it. There was not one of them hurt; but a little boy that was on the end had every one fall on him and it scared him pretty bad and bruised him a little, but he is practising to-day as usual."

Her aunt's horse by dint of much persuasion was taking some baby hurdles while the aunt hung on behind clinging to a strap, for the horse did not seem to care about having a person perched on his haunches, but he accepted it for the same reason that he had all the rest. But at last he was led from the ring and some one called "Dallie!" She jumped down from her tub, dropped off her long skirt, danced into the ring and up to a big white horse. She wore a short skirt over her dark bloomers and in her hand was a very weather-beaten little whip.

"I have tried a lot of others," she said, as she bent it, "but I cannot turn somersaults with any other. I am so used to this and the way it feels in my hand that I cannot get along with any other. I have lost this several times but some of the men always find it and bring it back to me."

Her horse, with its tightly checked head, waited for her and she felt the head strap with the air of an old professional.

Dallie stood up like a bit of thistle-down and, poised lightly on her horse, went riding around. First one of her feet and then the other went forward to balance, and then suddenly both went tight together and she took several preliminary leaps in the air to get herself limber. Having stretched her muscles, she gave a little cry. Three men, lined up together to catch her if she fell, got ready, and up and over in the air she went like a little human ball. The first time she did not land on the horse but in the ring. But after that she did her turn all right and was driven out to make room for others needing practice.

Cupid had picked the little horsewoman out for his mark in these early days of the circus, but so closely guarded was the secret that it was days before we knew that her heart had taken up its lodging in young Ledgett's breast, and his breast had become the cabinet of her affections. Shy glances and low and tender voices in secluded spots finally told a revealing tale and we watched the progress of the devotion with intense interest and some concern. We knew the stern traditional circus antipathy toward affairs of the kind and wondered whether the fixed opposition of the aunt could be overcome. No comrade was so disloyal and unchivalrous as to carry the story to those in authority, but soon the love-making conveyed itself to their very eyes. Then began a systematic effort to end it abruptly, and the memory of the courage and faith and hope which forced surrender to Hymen's cause will linger with us long.

The burden of obstructions was directed at the girl—he was too strong and self-reliant; and when her aunt was not advising against her conjugal plans, the ringmaster engaged himself in telling that marriage would jeopardize her future. So it was that between the prodigious shakings of the head and the love that absorbed her, Dallie grew thin and pale and unsteady in her work. Her judge of distance, so necessary in her dangerous aerial revolutions, became bad, and often she alighted on wooden ringbark or horse's head or tail when her feet should have been fixed to Gypsy's moving back. She became a bruised and humble maiden, but with purpose unwavering. Her aunt's vigilance was unrelaxing and unrelenting; she vowed that the two should not have each other's company.

To the casual circus goer, this determined disapproval of innocent attachment may seem brutal and unreasonable, but there are reasons underlying which those directly involved feel justify their course. It is the history of circus love affairs which progress during the active season that they impair performances. Once the yearning enters show persons, indolence and indifference characterize them in the ring. It is not a desire to oppress, but a warning instinct of professional deterioration, that causes sardonic smiles and harsh flings. To the relative who has acted as mother for years, the prospect of premature separation is naturally obnoxious.

It was not until summer was on the wane that we saw signs of approaching capitulation. Dallie had risen supreme over her temporary weakness and was again the skilful mistress of the ring. Fred, patient and artful, had won first an enduring place in the aunt's esteem and then her permission and encouragement. The management yielded before their combined eloquence.

So it was that one Sunday afternoon, Dallie, swaying under a great breadth of silk, and her sweetheart, awkward in encumbering black, but looking very proud and joyful, started hand in hand down the long road of life. A very glorious supper was served that evening in honor of the event. The owner gracefully proposed the health of the bride, and the tent resounded with the enthusiasm of the response. Fred expressed his thanks in well-put words, and Mrs. Fred blushed prettily in her happiness. And best of all, about the corners of the aunt's lip there rested a smile of pleasure, of approval and of contentment.

CHAPTER VII

THE MENAGERIE TENT

Into the menagerie tent, with its great variety of animals caged and unconfined, streams the open-mouthed human parade, stopping to comment and observe on its way to the "big top." The lions and tigers pace up and down their cages with hungry eyes that gleam in green and gold. They stare steadily through the iron bars but take no heed of the pigmy humans who stare back. There is something in those shining eyes that tells of thoughts far from the circus, perhaps of a jungle in far-off Asia. The insatiable elephant swings his greedy trunk tirelessly, and the black leopard sulks in the darkest corner of his den. Watching closely the scene in all its aspects is a jovial, deep-voiced man who urges the immediate necessity of securing advantageous seats under the adjoining canvas. He controls the peanut and lemonade privilege. Long experience has taught him all the arts and devices of his business. He appreciates that his sales will not begin in any volume until the audience is comfortably settled inside. Then he displays his commercial craftiness by overwhelming the big area with peanut and popcorn vendors. No lemonade is in evidence. Thirst comes on apace. Throats become dry and salty, and there is clamor for liquid. When its assuaging presence is finally seen in the hands of dozens of hawkers, the sale is invariably tremendous. If sudden rain comes on during the performance, he varies his sales with the disposal of umbrellas. He is ready for any meteorological condition.

He has been associated with red wagons and white canvas for many years, and there is no department of circus life in which he has not at some time excelled. As a clown his fame covered all parts of the country. He was, an old-time programme before me tells, "a grotesque, whimsical satirist. A wit brimful of ridiculously extravagant, fanciful mirth and eccentric humor, comic attitudes, funny songs, derisive sayings, quaint arguments and pleasant drolleries; entirely devoid of low jests and vulgar tricks and postures."

The monkey cage is the most popular institution in our menagerie tent. We have outgrown the "variety cage" of old days, which was a collection in one den of monkeys, pigs, cats, dogs and rabbits. It was an interesting collection, I suppose, to country people, but an insufferable nuisance to the showman. Circus monkeys die in droves. The show which starts the season with one hundred and fifty of the animals and returns to winter quarters with twenty-five is fortunate. The climatic changes act with quick fatality upon the sensitive creatures. Tuberculosis, animal doctors call the killing disease. There is always a bully in the cage and always an inmate ready to give battle for the honor. The privileges of the bully are alluring. He takes for himself the choicest morsels of food, chooses the most comfortable perch or corner, gives orders and demands instant obedience, and cuffs and bites and annoys his fellows until one, rendered desperate, turns and administers a thrashing and succeeds to the position.

The monkey cage at nightfall is a sure register of the degree of generosity of a community. In some towns they are gorged with food; the audience has fed them lavishly. Again, they give pleading indication of hunger; the place has probably a reputation for penuriousness. Those who believe in the Darwinian theory assert that the resemblance between the human race and the monkey is most marked in sick monkeys. Several scientists who watched our sick chimpanzee noticed many peculiarities of a child. It coughed like a child and made wry faces like one when asked to take medicine. Doctors felt its pulse and it received all the care and attention of a child of the rich.

A "MAN KILLER," PHOTOGRAPHED HALF AN HOUR AFTER HAVING SLAIN AN ANNOYER.

Natural history is one of the most interesting and absorbing of all studies, and the visitor to our menagerie finds much zoological gratification. The hippopotamus, sleeping or floundering in his tank, and raising his head at intervals above the surface of the water for the purpose of respiration, is never without a wondering audience. His is a harmless disposition and he is a pet with the animal keepers. His den is too small for the water to cover him completely and frequently he is scrubbed with soap. He enjoys the operation immensely unless the soapsuds enter his cavernous mouth, which surely is annoying enough to provoke the most mild-mannered being. His skin is of a dark reddish-brown color, full of cracks, chaps and cross-etchings, with dapplings of irregular dark spots, and is probably two inches thick. He is more than ten feet long and nearly six feet high. When he gives voice, the lions are humiliated and the tigers acknowledge defeat. It is a deafening kind of interrupted roar, between that of a bull and the braying of an elephant. His daily diet is bushels of potatoes, apples, carrots, oats, bran, hay and salt. Keepers say that the only hippopotami born in captivity are in the zoo of one of the big cities. Ignorance permitted the first one which saw the light to die. Keepers feared to put it in the water, thinking it would drown, and tried to nurse it with a bottle. It was dead in ten days. Then it was decided not to interfere when the mother brought forth its next young. The result was the discovery that it nursed under water. The first genuine hippopotamus ever seen in America was exhibited by Barnum in his New York museum in August, 1861. He advertised the animal extensively and ingeniously as the "great behemoth of the Scriptures," and thousands, including many biblical students, flocked to see it.

Circus people will travel miles into the presence of a giraffe. They want the animal with the elongated neck to rub their hand with its tongue. They say that good luck is sure to follow the operation. The privilege is one rarely accorded, for giraffes are very costly and delicate, and, though popular menagerie inmates, are infrequently seen nowadays. The first one born in captivity in America saw the light of day in Cincinnati on October 20, 1889. It was five feet high. Daisy, measuring eighteen feet from the ground to the tips of her ears, and the last giraffe then on exhibition with any travelling show, was killed during a voyage to Europe—a lurch of the ship broke her neck.

Circus owners are vainly searching the jungles of India and the wilds of Africa for rhinoceroses. There are none in the open markets and the world's visible supply is limited to twelve specimens. The market value of the beast ranged from $4,000 to $5,000 until the present shortage set in. Now a large circus would willingly pay many times that sum. The rhinoceros has always been a problem to animal keepers, for captivity generally results in early death. He is a beast so essentially of the wilds that all efforts at breeding in captivity have failed. Old showmen remember the attempt to take performing liberties with one of the spike-nosed monsters in a small town in Illinois in 1872. He killed two men, upset four dens of animals, tore down a museum tent, stampeded people for blocks and finally brought up in a vacant house, the door of which stood open. No fixed desire to exhibit a rhinoceros has ever since been displayed.

To many persons who go to a circus there is probably nothing that causes more wonder than to see the keepers of the lions, tigers, leopards, panthers and other wild beasts sitting in the cages among them, patting them on their ugly heads, slapping them on their saliva-dripping jowls, or fearlessly lashing them with their whips if necessary. Mastery expresses better than training what the keepers have accomplished with the beasts.

"There is a tremendous amount of work to be done in winter quarters, of which the public knows nothing," explained our keeper, as he surveyed the scene in the menagerie tent early one August evening. "We are getting new wild animals all the time, and as they come to us there is not a man living who would dare go into the cages with them. During the winter we have to break those beasts so that we can handle them on the road. When they come to us they have thick leather collars around their necks, with heavy chains attached. The beasts are then more savage than they were before capture, that having served only to bring out all that is ugly in them. They will spit and growl at anybody who comes near their cage, and jump at the bars until they exhaust themselves. We begin to teach them manners the very day we get them, and they take a lesson in etiquette every day after that until the show starts out. My men catch the end of the chain fastened to the collar and secure it in such a manner to the bars that the beast can move only a short distance. Then I take a stout rawhide whip and strong club and enter the cage. I take a chair and sit down in a corner. The instant I get in, the beast will give a roar and spring for me. I would be torn to shreds if I were within reach; but the chain holds and instead of getting at me, the lion, tiger, panther or leopard is brought up with a shock that sends him in a heap to the floor and I give him a lash with the rawhide.

REHEARSING IN WINTER QUARTERS.

"The beast is at me again in an instant; again he goes down and again I lash him. I always keep the club handy, but never use it unless it is absolutely necessary. I keep drawing my chair a little closer to the animal as this goes on until I get so close he can touch me with his nose but cannot bite me. Then I just sit there and talk to him and you would be surprised at the power the human voice will finally be made to exercise over wild beasts. They seem to understand much that is said to them.

"While I am talking just out of reach of their teeth," he went on, "if they get ugly and attempt to spring at me I give them the rawhide. I keep this up, and after a dozen or fifteen lessons they get so they only snarl and growl at my entrance to the cage. As soon as I think it is safe I try the beasts without a chain. It is a little ticklish business at first but I have plenty of help ready for the first effort. If it is a success the first time, you generally have your beast mastered, although once in a while a brute that has been tractable enough will break out and go for his keeper. We had such a case once when an experienced lion tamer was clawed by a lioness and nearly killed. We usually cut the claws of the cat species, however. Lions will not stay in the same cage with tigers. We tried this once, putting a lioness in with a Bengal tiger. There was a fierce fight and the lioness nearly killed the Bengal."

Our keeper takes very little stock in the theory of the power of the human eye over wild beasts. The organ plays an insignificant part, he thinks; it is the power of the man behind the eye and the qualifications he possesses that are efficacious.

"It is a pretty thing to say, and that is all," he said. "The man who wants to subdue a wild beast has to be fearless and go about his task in a courageous way, and of course the eye plays its part. The man who attempted to handle a wild beast that was not chained, with nothing else than a fearless eye would be in a pretty bad hole, though. What the man must have is a good heart, plenty of pluck and lots of sand. The secret of successfully handling wild beasts is to become imbued with a confidence that all wild beasts are really cowardly, especially if they belong to the cat family. If you are not afraid and you know how to do it, it is easy enough.

"A circus man once determined to put the question whether the human eye has power over wild animals to the test. Approaching a large ostrich he gazed fixedly at it, and to his delight the mesmeric glance seemed to meet with instant success. The bird crouched and flapped its wings nervously. Some hours later, however, the man's body was found with the ostrich alternately sitting and jumping upon it. The negro guide of a circus expedition, it is told, was more successful, although there is some doubt as to whether it was the power of the eye that gave him victory. He surprised two lion cubs at play and began to play with them. They liked it so much that when he would take his departure they refused to let him go. Their cries of enjoyment finally brought the mother lioness. The negro was paralyzed with fear, and kept his eyes glued to those of the lioness. Man and beast kept steadily watching each other. The lioness moved around the negro several times but he never shifted his gaze. Several times the lioness crouched as if to spring, but finally after what seemed an age to the negro she called her cubs to her side and disappeared in the forest. This is the story brought home from Africa.

"A man once experimented with a wildcat in our circus, and only the bars of the cage prevented him from being badly scratched for his pains. As soon as he looked into the eyes of the wildcat the animal sprang fiercely at him.

"Some interesting experiments were made at our winter quarters in Bridgeport one year with the object of ascertaining the exact influence of music on animals. That animals like to hear a violin played seems to be clearly proved. A zoologist played in the menagerie many times, and found that the music pleased them. A puma, at the sound of the violin, stretched himself at full length in his cage and listened quietly as long as the music was soft and low, but the moment it became loud and fast he sprang to his feet, lashed his sides with his tail and began to pace nervously up and down his cage. A jaguar at the sound of lively music showed great uneasiness, but became quiet when soft music was played. He thrust his paws through the bars of the cage to detain the violinist. On leopards the music made hardly any impression. A lioness and three cubs seemed somewhat disturbed, but as soon as the player started to go to the next cage they came forward and lay down. He then played soft music which seemed to please them. He followed it with a lively dance, at the first sound of which the cubs sprang up and gambolled wildly about the cage. On the other hand, two striped hyenas, when they heard the music, drew back to the other end of their cage and tried to get out through the bars.

"I remember well the year 1889," he continued, "because then the question of electrocuting, instead of hanging, prisoners condemned to die came up. A party of scientists came on to our winter quarters and conducted a series of electrical experiments upon the animals. Mr. Bailey placed the entire menagerie at the service of the scientists, and twenty of us keepers assisted in the work. The instruments employed were a powerful battery of forty-two Leclanche cells and a resistance box of one hundred thousand ohms. The experiments began at eleven o'clock in the morning and continued until nightfall.

"The first animal experimented with was a savage baboon, which fought furiously before he was tied. He bit one keeper severely and tore the clothing off another. A sponge, that was used as the end of one wire, was forced into his mouth. A second sponge was fastened on one of his paws. A current of two cells was then passed through the simian and was promptly resented by a fierce attempt to break his bonds and escape. The baboon's irritation increased with the current until twenty-eight cells had been used. When forty cells had been used, the animal became lethargic and almost comatose, looking for all the world like a man overcome by strong drink. The highest point of resistance was eight thousand ohms, a surprisingly large figure. When finally released, the baboon became wild with rage and attacked the nearest keeper, inflicting a dozen scratches on him. A tame seal was next operated on. It allowed the experts to fasten one roll of copper wire around its neck and a second around its tail flippers. The moment the current was applied it snapped viciously in every direction. The savants sprang right and left, upsetting chairs and writing materials in their haste to get out of reach. When the current was increased the seal gnawed at the wires and succeeded in disengaging itself from both. The resistance could not be ascertained on account of its wet coat acting as a conductor to the electric fluid.

"The gnu or horned horse, did not take kindly to science. When one of the savants entered its cage it attacked him so savagely, that three keepers were obliged to go to his assistance. The animal showed a resistance of eleven thousand ohms and seemed paralyzed the moment the current was turned on. The small monkeys behaved very much like little children. The moment they felt the current they screamed and seemed to be undergoing agony. When the wires were removed, they appeared puzzled and three of them took up the electrodes as if to study them. A large blue monkey was so interested that when released he seized the large sponge and began to tear it apart as if to see what it contained that hurt him so. The monkeys offered a resistance of from five thousand to seven thousand ohms. The hippopotamus and sea lion took the full force of the current without wincing; but a dog, after having a moderate current passed through his brain, showed signs of hydrophobia and had to be killed. The wild carnivora showed much sensitiveness to the electric current, manifesting every symptom of rage and distress when only a single cell was employed. A wolf to which a mild current was applied, stood upon its haunches and cried piteously.

"But the elephants proved the star attractions. They actually enjoyed the sensation in every instance, except when a strong current was passed through the trunk. When only a few cells were employed, the huge beasts did not seem to observe the fact, but when the full battery was employed, they rubbed their legs together, caressed savant and keeper alike and squealed their pleasure. No odder sight was ever seen than an elephant with mouth wide open, with one scientist holding a sponge to the huge tongue and a second another to the root of his tail, and manifesting every sign of glee.

"The manner in which animals endure pain always awakens our sympathies. Horses in battle are a striking example of power of endurance and unyielding courage. After the first stinging pain of the wound, they make no sound, but bear their agony with mute, wondering endurance. Elephants also suffer agonies without flinching. When they are shot in a vital spot they sink down on the ground with a low cry, and silently pass away. A dog will go for days with a broken leg without complaint, and a wounded cat will crawl to some quiet place and brood silently over agonies which humans could not endure. A stricken deer will go to some thick wood and there in pitiful submission await the end. Lions, tigers and other beasts will do the same. Seldom do they give utterance to cries of pain. Cattle will meet the thrust of the butcher's knife without a sound, and a wild dove, with shot from a hunter's gun burning in its tender flesh, will fly to some high bough or lie on the ground to die, and no sound will be heard save the dripping of its life blood upon the leaves. The eagle, stricken high in air, will struggle to the last, but there will be no sound of pain, and the proud defiant look will not leave the eyes until the lids close over them and shut out the sunlight they love so well."

Sunday is fast-day in the menagerie tent, and every occupant, caged or uncaged, knows when the day arrives. When the week-day feeding hour—five o'clock in the afternoon—approaches, not one of the animals betrays the feeling of eager desire on Sunday which characterizes them all the other six days. They understand instinctively that there will be no meal. Then on Monday the "cat" animals begin to pace their cages nervously and peer through the bars awaiting the coming of the keepers. They are well aware that liver, which they relish keenly and which keeps them in good physical condition, will be the food. The Sunday abstinence is deemed by the trainers an aid to good health, as copying to some extent the habit of beasts in their native haunts, where food is not obtainable every day. There is little sickness in the menagerie. The animals are studied closely and given assiduous attention if the slightest indisposition is manifested.

CHAPTER VIII

LIFE WITH THE PERFORMERS

The art of seating the audience in the big tent plays a prominent part in the receipts of the day. "Fill the highest rows first," is the instruction forced upon each usher, and censure or dismissal is the penalty of disobedience. By skilful and systematic arrangement of the crowds, it is possible to utilize every inch of seating space in the vast enclosure. Indifferent or careless performance of the duty leaves the tent, to the casual observer, packed to completion, but in reality here and there are spots not occupied. Hence all ingenuity must be brought to bear to prevent this condition and its consequent financial loss, for the sale of tickets stops when no more seats are available. Sometimes a prosperous day has not been confidently expected and the management orders a four- instead of the usual five-centre-pole tent raised. The difference in seating capacity is several hundred. Then, but not often, for circus foresight is keen, people flock to the lot in thousands and there is no room for their accommodation. The owner is shame and mortification personified.

On the hippodrome track one of the clowns, clad in sober black and looking to be all he represents, waits with imitation camera and tripod for victims. He is an experienced master of human nature. With exaggerated politeness and scrupulous care of detail he poses unsuspecting new-comers, to the boisterous amusement of those already seated. Sweethearts stand in affectionate attitude, mightily pleased and unsuspecting, while he pretends to impress their likeness upon photographic plates. Sometimes he turns their faces from him, tells them not to move until instructed, and then moves quietly away. Very infrequently they take the joke seriously. When anger and retaliation are manifested, he is agile enough to escape punishment.

A boy sings on the topmost seats. His voice is powerful, but pure and sweet, and the tent is filled with the sounds of approval when he finishes. The musical director discovered him in Rochester, N. Y., and has great hopes for his professional future.

The military band is discoursing popular selections, and the equestrian director makes a last critical survey of the network of suspended bars, trapezes, rings, perches and wires. Finishing touches are being added to the "loop-the-loop" apparatus. A score of men have been putting it together since early morning. Now the band is at the dressing-room exit and the cornet sounds a melodious call. The inaugural tournament is on, comprising, the press agent is telling his guests, "spectacular pageantry, zoologic, equestric, hippodromatic and aerial elements, indicative of the limitless resources of this colossal consolidation of circus chieftains, collection of celebrities and congress of champions; a comprehensive, kaleidoscopic and illustrative review upon the ellipse of the hippodrome, upon the two stages and in the three rings."

Then the clowns' carol, the herds of trained elephants and the circus performance that is familiar to the young and old. The ringmaster's whip cracks merrily; ponies and dogs show the results of patient teaching; slack wire equilibrists, head balancers and daring horizontal bar heroes are innumerable; there are graceful flights upon flying trapeze and swinging rings; living classic statuary pleases the eye; hurdle riding, a hazardous form of equestrianism, gives the audience a thrill; prancing thoroughbreds engage in a cakewalk, and the clowns burlesque it; a crowd of acrobats and jugglers fill the rings simultaneously, while a septette of men and women engage in fancy and trick bicycle riding, and the most intrepid wheelman rides down a ladder which stretches to the dome of the canvas; a performing bear shows almost human intelligence, and some one dressed like a monster rooster evokes general mirth; a young man, standing on the pedals of a single wheel with no support save his nerve, makes his perilous journey up and down a spiral arrangement, which has a curious effect upon the snare drum; an eighteen-year-old girl turns somersaults upon a moving white horse's back, and the onlookers read that she is the only one of her sex accomplishing the feat.

So the show progresses to the rushing hippodrome races, contests between women on fiery thoroughbreds, double standing Roman bareback races, tandem hurdle races, jockey races, pony races with monkey jockeys, clowns in comical competition, and the breath-taking chariot race. It is now that the country crowd perhaps gets a thrill that is denied the New York city audience. In Madison Square Garden the hippodrome track is dry and firm and smooth and true. The country course offers none of these conditions. No time is granted to make it perfect. And so it is that sometimes there is a wild cry from rider or driver, a confused heap of hoofs, legs, wheels and dust, breathless silence from the thousands of onlookers and then, generally, a loud burst of applause as horse and human struggle to their feet, not seriously damaged. The danger of disaster is especially great when the four fleet horses are dashing with the heavy, low Roman chariots. Great skill is required to prevent collision or collapse on the abrupt course; and rough, uneven grounds make serious strain upon the vehicle. The accidents seldom have disastrous endings. I remember vividly when an axle broke in a Pennsylvania town. The woman driver jumped and escaped with a sprained wrist. The band instantly stopped its thumping. The horses, racing madly and unguided to the finish post came to an abrupt standstill. The audience, on a verge of a panic, resumed their seats, marvelling. They did not understand, that as a precautionary measure against just such accidents, the fiery animals are trained to run with the music. They have been taught not to move rapidly until the band begins and to stop whenever its melody ceases.

It will be observed that the women who rush around the hippodrome track in the jockey races ride in an opposite direction from that of the other sex, and the reason is not apparent to the lay visitor. The explanation is that thus their feet swing on the horse's side not exposed to the supporting quarter-pole, as would be the case did they follow the course of the men. Disregard of this precautionary measure has resulted in serious injury in many circuses, for the circus woman makes light of danger in many forms which would appall her unprofessional sister. The natural route is the men's, and she would take it every time did the equestrian director permit.

RING "STARS" LINED UP FOR INSPECTION.

Of course, most skilled performers "stall." That is, in the execution of a particularly dangerous or difficult feat, they pretend to barely escape a serious fall or make an unsuccessful attempt at accomplishment. It gives the audience an exaggerated idea of the extreme peril or difficulty of the undertaking, and ensures an outburst of applause when finally triumphantly done. It is a sidelight on the mild vanity of the circus man, but incidentally serves a commercial purpose, for he knows that public approval carries with it renewal of engagement at no smaller salary.

Nearly all on the list of circus performances have inherited their strength and skill. They have been literally born to the arena. Some of them represent the third and fourth generations of famous circus families. The boys and girls of our circus, comprising two tiny concert dancers, a smart young bicycle rider, several acrobats and gymnasts and two Japanese boys, are a modest, healthy, honest party of playmates whose parents find time each day to hear lessons and give advice in manners and morals. They are "chums" in all the word implies, and an occasional clash with words or fists always ends without the call for parental adjustment and serves to cement the juvenile friendship. Of young men and women, those who have not yet reached their majorities, we have half a dozen, all of whom have conspicuous parts in the show. One of the girls, a skilled acrobat, took up riding recently and bids fair to achieve fame, the veterans say. The act does not interfere with her other performance and she is in receipt of a handsome income. The most finished tumbler among the lads is a boy who also participates in a wire-walking act. In this performance he is disguised as a girl, for the feminine sex always lends interest to any feat. The deception is perfect, but it was very annoying to the management and embarrassing to the youth when his blonde wig dropped off one afternoon and he stood revealed in his masculinity. So it is with a "family" who do a graceful and dangerous aerial act. The youngest member of the troupe is a boy, although appearance indicates the other sex. They are both eagerly biding the time when age will do away with the disguise.

The training of these children begins almost at birth. Indeed, in the vast majority of cases there is the powerful effect of heredity, which exercises an influence upon the child and helps it to overcome obstacles to others well-nigh impossible. The chief effort is to create courage and daring, to develop those qualities where they already exist. The lungs are expanded and broadened by hearty exercise, and the muscles are hardened and developed by athletic work. At the same time it has been found by the modern gymnast that the body, to perform this extraordinary work, must be well nourished. The necessity for a clear head, a steady eye and unflinching hand requires that the brain shall likewise be well nourished; so the education of the little pupils is not neglected; indeed, many a gymnast has mental abilities often lacking in the ordinary man. He has to understand some geometry and mathematics, else how can he calculate the exact distance of a jump, a fall, a somersault? He very often is the inventor of his own apparatus and this has to be exact in shape, size and strength. The suppleness of the limbs and joints comes from long practice, not, as is usually thought, from straining the soft joints of a child. The result of such straining would be weakness, not strength. Only those whose business it is know or understand what can be done with those joints, how much strain they will bear and which will endure the greatest strain. When to hold on and when to let go are important items, too, in an acrobat's training. These can be learned only when young. It is natural for a child to "catch at something" when it thinks it is falling. It must be taught to do the catching only at precisely the right moment, and to turn at the instant when required.

In these days, the net is an element of safety in all mid-air feats. But so fearless and confident do gymnasts become that they hardly know and certainly do not notice whether it is in place. There is a piece of apparatus largely used among circus riders when training or learning new feats called the "mecanique." It consists of a belt, which goes around the waist of the performer, to which is attached a strong, elastic rope, which is again fastened to a wooden, gibbet-like arm. The tyro knows that he cannot possibly fall beyond the length of the rope and that, therefore, no matter how many times he fails, he cannot by any possibility come to physical grief. The use of this machine is deprecated by some performers as reducing the nerve training to a minimum. It is, however, in great favor with all whose nerves are already steadied by experience and who are trying new tricks. In the case of women and children the "mecanique" is very frequently employed.

There is no phase of work that requires more patient and faithful study, more steadiness of nerve or a greater command of the muscles than feats of balancing on trapeze, rings and slack wire. To balance well, one must be systematically developed, and each muscle must be ready to act instantly and do its work with certainty. The legs must be strong and firm to sustain the body in its various poses. The back must be sinewy, so that the recovery may be made quickly and the upright maintained without a chance of failure, and the arms and hands must be hard and strong; for when a man, falling from a trapeze, grasps at the bar, he must catch it and hold to it if he desires to emerge unhurt. Balancing on the slack wire is essentially different from trapeze balancing. On the slack wire the balance must be kept by working the body from the waist down, and is mainly done with the legs. It is the reverse on the trapeze, where the legs must be kept rigid and the balance worked from the leg up. The slack wire is harder to learn at first than the trapeze, as it is radically different from a person's natural balance, which is kept more with the arms and body and less with the legs.

The triple somersault has slain its scores, yet as long as men tumble over elephants in the circus, and as long as springboards are made, the acrobats will be trying to accomplish this most difficult of feats. There have been acrobats who have done it. They are dead now. They were carried out of the ring to a hospital immediately thereafter, and lived for the various periods of from one to three days. There have been men who have asserted that they can turn the triple. They are generally the acrobats who have left the circus ring forever and are devoting the last years of their lives to the sale of cigars or some other stirring occupation. The men who have followed the circus all their lives say that no man has ever turned the triple from a springboard and lived to boast of his triumph. The triple somersault is done from a flying trapeze, but it is simply a series of revolutions in the air as the performer drops. Even then it should be called two and a half revolutions, for the acrobat falls on his back in a net and depends upon the rebound to hurl him to his feet. He can make these two revolutions and a half from a springboard, sometimes, with the difference that nine hundred and ninety-nine times out of a thousand he alights on his head or on the back of his neck which brings instant death. A man who even falls that way in a net is a subject for the coroner.

It is circus tradition that in 1842, when even the double somersault was deemed a difficult and dangerous feat, a performer tried the triple turn. It happened in Mobile, Alabama, and the rash acrobat broke his neck. W. J. Hobbes, a tumbler, was killed attempting the trick in London four years later. John Amor, a Pennsylvania circus leaper, who was a famous double somersault revolver, paid with his life for his ambition in 1859. He was travelling with an English circus, essayed the death-dealing act, struck on his forehead and died.

The somersault, whether it be single or double, is a feat which requires the most assiduous practice and the most accurate calculation. The first thing which the tumbler learns is to jump from a springboard. The sensation of springing through the air is an uncanny one. Next is the "stock" somersault, which consists of merely springing up in the air and slowly, and with practically no muscular exertion, turning over. The motion is so slow that the spectators hardly realize that the man has revolved. Then begins the drill for the real somersault. The acrobat learns the "tuck," which consists of grasping both legs tightly half way between the knee and ankle and pressing them closely together. At the same time the acrobat puts the muscles of his shoulders and back into play. This muscular force acts like the balance weight of the wheel. It aids him to complete the revolution. The taking of the "tuck" requires the nicest calculation. The acrobat must wait until he has sprung as far in the air as the force of the springboard or his legs will carry him. If he "tucks" too soon he will fall like a coffee sack. If he waits until too late he finds himself cast, a human wheel at a dead centre. He is likely to have broken bones in either case in spite of carpet or mattress. The double somersault requires more muscular force. The trained acrobat knows exactly where he is at every point in the revolution. He has a strange sense which makes him feel it. It is when he summons his almost exhausted energies for a third turn that he feels like a ship without a rudder. Harry Costello, Wm. Kinkead, John Armstrong, Arthur Mohring, and "Little Bob" Hanlon, well-known circus performers, have broken their necks and died in executing the double somersault within a score of years.

The dressing-rooms—the "green room" of the circus—are as convenient to the centre of the tent as the topography of the lot will permit. Passing through the canvas connection, the women of the show enter quarters to the left and the men's accommodations are on the other side. Between, stand the horses and wagons and other "property" which for various reasons cannot be stored near the rings. Very cosy and comfortable are the two canvas compartments, although room is at a premium. Trunks replace chairs, and mirrors are of a dimension to discourage vanity. The process of "making up" is a laborious, and tedious undertaking, but accepted as one of the conditions which are unavoidable. Of cold water there is a plenty, and soap and towels abound. Naphtha lights furnish illumination. Electric experiments have never been successful.

The music of the band furnishes the circus man's cue. He knows by its brazen notes when to leave the dressing-room for the ring. If the musical director changes an air, the dressing-room inmates must be thoroughly informed to avoid delay and confusion. No performer is permitted to leave until the entire show is over. The danger of accident in the ring is never absent, and as many do several "turns" others must be ready if one becomes incapacitated. When the nights grow cold in the early and late season, the chill air which penetrates the canvas would drive any but the hardy circus folk to a sick-bed. Their trained systems are equal to all demands the elements put forward, however, and a cough or a cold are almost unknown. A miserable enough place it is when the rain falls freely. Scant as is the dressing-room protection, the journey to and from the rings is infinitely worse. Performers return to their trunks wet in the feet and generally bestrewed with drops from the head down. Pretty costumes are spotted and the effect is very depressing. There is peril to life and limb, too, when bars and trapezes and rings and other apparatus becomes drenched. Hands may slip, feet may not hold, a horse may stumble, and there are numberless other chances of misfortune. The equestrian director decides whether or not the possibility of disaster is too great for the act. If he deems the risk not too venturesome, the performer accepts cheerfully, no matter what is his own conviction. Sometimes he enters upon the duty with grim forebodings as to the outcome, for he appreciates that perhaps the director, in his desire not to disappoint the audience, has imposed a critical undertaking. The circus concert offers opportunity for a display of talents other than those presented in the ring. Many performers with nimble foot or tuneful voice add to their incomes by this extra work.

Circus performers are persons of large and unwearied charity and compassion. No comrade is deserted in affliction or distress. Contributions of money and sympathy flow in upon him, and none fails to subscribe. If the situation requires more money than one circus is able to provide, word of the need is sent to friends with other similar organizations and there is always prompt and ready response. I know of a dozen invalids who are to-day being supported solely by the liberal benevolence of comrades.

Two benevolent societies are with the Barnum & Bailey circus, the B.O.S.S. and the Tigers. Each makes a weekly collection from the members and pays $15.00 weekly to the sick or disabled. Last year $9,000 was collected and $8,000 disbursed. The balances remained in the treasurers' hands for this year.

Many of the people of the circus accumulate competences after a few years' work, and there is no reason why all who live prudently should not soon be financially independent. Their expenses of travel, board and bed are all borne by the management, and other requirements of a circus campaign are few and small. It is a common practice with some to draw only a small share of their salaries each week. The accumulated balance awaits them in the money wagon at the close of the season. Then, there is the "mother" of the circus with whom many of the unmarried men and the boys deposit a weekly stipend. No plea, however piteous, will force her to disgorge, they know, until the last stand has been played. Then the amassed wealth is handed to them with a parting kindly injunction to be moderate through the winter and return next year with as much unspent as consistent. This interest in his welfare has started many a circus man on the road to prosperity and fortune.

The "mother" is one of the most interesting characters of the circus. Her life is devoted particularly to the welfare of the woman performers under tents. Her official duty is as matron of the women's dressing-room. She it is who supervises their wardrobe, mends sudden breaches in the tarlatan and bespangled skirts and cares for her charges in case of illness or accident. Should an equestrienne fall from her horse, it is the "circus mother" who brings the cup of black coffee, which is the only stimulant ever given to gymnasts and acrobats in such an emergency.

At night, after the performance, she presides over the performers' luncheon of sandwiches and tea, which the circus women enjoy in the sleeping car. In short, she is a general chaperon, hospital nurse, friend and counsellor in one. Our "mother's" long experience in circus life has made her familiar with every detail of the business and she knows what to do, without any prompting, whenever any emergency arises. Men and women alike come to her with the petty troubles that are bound to occur in the uncertain and strenuous existence they lead. She is cheery, sympathetic or admonitory as the occasion may require, and no one leaves her presence without being the better for having come into contact with the motherly matron. It is an axiom among circus people that the good-will of the "mother" is equivalent to lasting favor with the management, and that to incur her ill-will is to stand an imminent risk of losing an engagement.

A large part of her duty is the care of the circus wardrobe, and during the winter she devotes her entire time to it. With her deft fingers and the judicious use of naphtha she makes old circus costumes look like new. Trappings which are worn by the animals in the grand entry are all made by the "mother" and her assistants during the idle winter season. She is as expert at cutting a pattern for the costumes of the animals as a Fifth avenue modiste is at cutting those for her smart clientele. She is, in short, the Worth of circusland. Although nearly sixty years old, she is as lively as a woman half her age.

The domestic instinct is very strong among the circus women for the reason that they are deprived of home life, a great part of every year. It finds an outlet in many little ways, one of which is an appeal to the chef in charge of the dining car to be allowed to bake a cake. If he is in a mood to give them permission they are pleased as children, and begin a hunt for eggs and milk. The train may be standing just outside of some village, and they run out and buy the things and come back and cook as though it were the greatest fun in the world. When their cake or pie is done, it is passed through the car, and no matter how small it may be, there is always a bit for everyone. Sometimes the cook is ill-tempered and won't let them fuss around, but that doesn't always stop them. It isn't at all unusual for them to go to one of the houses along near the track and ask the woman who lives there to let them use her kitchen. Almost always they get permission and afterwards pay for it.

They sew, too, and many do exceedingly pretty fancy work. They don't have to keep their circus clothes in order. The "circus mother" does that, but they do all the mending of personal garments, and besides keep some sort of pickup work on hand. There isn't a home of a circus woman that is not furnished with the covers of some sort she has made during the season. One seldom sees a circus woman in a city after the season is over. She flees from it. She detests the noise and bustle, and, almost without exception, they all live in little country towns, where they practise during the winter, go early to bed and are in fine condition when the season opens.

I know that it is a common thing to believe that a circus woman has no modesty, but the impression is a mistaken one. She can dress as she does and perform, and still be a perfectly good, pure woman. That is because no town has any identity to her, nor any person any individuality. It makes no difference to her whether the show is in New York City or Kalamazoo. There is simply a performance to be given, and she is not playing to any one person. There is no "he" in the audience who may be attracted to take her out to supper afterwards. He wouldn't have the chance to speak to her, if he wanted to, and if she seems to him an earth-born fairy, she never knows it. No women could live more protected lives. The performance isn't over until eleven o'clock, and all must be in the cars of the circus train by midnight, when the cars are usually locked for the night; and when one remembers that a circus woman is almost invariably married, and that her husband is with her, it can be appreciated that the moral standard of the profession is high. Most of the circus women support families, and their leisure between performances is spent in sewing—perhaps garments for younger children at home, or, as a matter of economy, for themselves; for they save every possible penny, finding incentive and practical aid in the fact that they need not consider the expense of living in the necessary outlay.

After the night performance, they return to their private cars, which are by that time prepared to start for another town as soon as the tents and other paraphernalia are aboard. Week after week of this routine, as regularly carried out as the work of a factory, requires physical stamina as well as the actual gymnastic or acrobatic circus faculty, for which a clear brain is the most requisite. These things are not maintained except by regular living. The motto of the circus acrobat, therefore, might be "plain living and high jumping." Beneath the white canvas, as under the brick and iron of city office buildings, there is no room for those who complain. "Headaches" and similar excuses for a non-appearance must for disciplinary reasons be frowned upon by the equestrian director—the stage manager of the circus. It is the "circus mother" who pleads with him to excuse the women who are not able to appear. She it is to whom they go with griefs and complaints and upon whose sympathy in their concern they may rely.

Frivolity, even in the innocuous guise of a waiting maid, is discouraged in circus life, and no woman performer, be she ever so celebrated, is allowed to carry a handmaiden to aid in dressing her. "No room for 'em," is the terse but eloquent excuse of the management.

Circuses of the better class look after the welfare of their woman performers with a surprising regard to detail. They are provided with a special car in which they live while on the road, except when the show plays a three-night or week's stand; in that case they are quartered in a hotel. How very comfortable their travelling quarters may be they are nevertheless pleased when an opportunity is had to spend a few days in a room which affords sufficient space to allow of unpacking and repacking trunks, for in one-night stands the trunk containing personal belongings is never moved except from car to lot. Woman riders frequently own their own horses. It is indeed considered a breach of circus etiquette, or more particularly speaking a lowering of one's "caste" to be content to ride an animal owned by some one else. The sharp little vibrant "clucks," with which the equestrienne commands her horse in the ring, are "cues" which he understands as well as he does the swaying of the ringmaster's whip from left to right, or the pressure of his rider's satin slipper. Each of these is a suggestion to his memory that brings instant response in some change of movement.

The disadvantage under which a circus woman "makes up" would drive an actress to despair. She sits upon a small stool before the stationary mirror in the upraised lid of the trunk, and "makes up" as best she can in the big dressing tent. There are perhaps thirty other women in the tent, and a wardrobe mistress in charge, prepared to mend suddenly acquired rents in emergencies. The use of alcohol for spirit lamps is not allowed unless with a special permit from the "mother." Many of the woman acrobats, gymnasts and jugglers are foreign. They have homes abroad, perhaps, and work industriously in leisure hours to beautify them. One woman who travelled last season with us completed during the tour an entire bed set of renaissance lace, cover and pillow shams. This same woman who is one of a troupe of acrobats, when twitted for her "stinginess," was wont to reply: "Well, it is another brick in my house—very dollar I save." She was buying a home for her mother and sister.

PRACTISING TRICKS IN THE OPEN.

Any one who witnesses the performance of these professional female athletes must marvel at the strength, skill and endurance that a woman is capable of. There are on both sides of the Atlantic more than two thousand women who earn their living in this way, and of these nearly one half are found in America. They like the West best; for they tell you the Westerner is the most ardent admirer of muscle and nerve as displayed by the gentler sex. The women like their business. They have no special dietary. They eat when they feel like it; eat heartily, too, and of anything they crave. Their remuneration varies from fifty to one hundred and fifty dollars a week. The best of them and, of course, the few, command the latter sum.

A woman performer with whom I talked one afternoon gave it as her opinion that women are more proficient as animal trainers than men. She said: "One need not seek far for a reason for this. In the first place, women are more patient, and it is quite a mistaken idea to suppose that rough methods are necessary in training animals. One sees many more woman animal trainers abroad than in this country, but a number of them have been celebrated in the United States. I think it is the mother instinct in women which enables them to command the obedience of animals. It is a well-known fact among circus people that monkeys are particularly fond of women. Horses, too, are readily trained by women.

"Some years ago I trained successfully a number of sheep, supposedly the stupidest of animals. I cannot say that I found them overweaningly intelligent, but with much patience, the virtue which I insist makes a woman capable as an animal trainer, I succeeded in teaching them a series of tricks both original and clever, such as are usually performed by a dog circus. Dogs and horses have the best memories, though some trainers contend that the elephant has. A dog or horse will respond to a nod or the slightest swaying motion of a whip from side to side. Elephants, being more ponderous of body, naturally require more time to train."

Few people distinguish between the gymnasts and acrobats of a circus, yet there is a distinction with a decided difference. The acrobat is he who tumbles and turns somersaults, and usually "starts the show" by running from a springboard and jumping over the wide backs of elephants in line. The gymnast is an aerial artist, and his work has little in common with that of the other performer. Some people, according to an authority on circus matters, are born with a balance. Presence of mind has not only to be a habit but an exact science, as it were, with the man or woman performer who would master the art of the flying ring. This is one of the reasons for the abstemiousness of the circus fraternity. No drugs or alcohol are permitted inside the circus tent. This is a law the violation of which means inevitable dismissal for any performer. Perhaps the very obvious necessity for its enforcement is at the same time the reason why it is so seldom broken. Performers must needs be springy of step, clear of head, keen of eye and sound of liver.

Perhaps few in a circus audience who have many times admired the graceful gesticulations of the tight rope and slack rope walkers realize the utility of the small Japanese umbrella which they wield with apparently careless grace. As a matter of fact, the umbrella and other paraphernalia thrown to them by the attendants and which they manipulate for no apparent reason save that of adding effectiveness to the act, are in reality used for balancing purposes. Many a wire walker has been saved from perhaps fatal accident by a dexterous swerving of the light parasol from right to left, readjusting the balance just in the nick of time.

Most of the circuses abroad are enclosed indoor affairs, and as the buildings in which such attractions are seen are of much greater height than anything we have in this country, the opportunity for daring gymnastic acts is far greater than here. At the Crystal Palace, the Olympia and the Royal Aquarium and also at the Alhambra, many feats are performed which it would be impossible to duplicate here. Children are oftener seen as acrobats and gymnasts in the old country than in America. They begin to train as early as three years of age and many tots of six and seven are wonderfully accomplished circus performers, in lands where the Children's Society holds not sway. These children are in many instances apprenticed out to old performers who train them, and are repaid in return by their services for a certain number of years.

Few of the members of the so-called acrobatic families bear any individual relationship to one another, and the name taken by the troupe is usually that of the trainer or leading acrobat.

Of late years costumes for acrobats have changed considerably. It used to be the fashion to wear tights and blouses which would be as little impedimental as possible to the free swing of the body. Now, however, the latest acrobatic actors imported from Europe are affecting evening dress, the women in décolleté gowns, full-skirted, and the men in the black and white habiliments prescribed by convention for dress occasions. Needless to say it is much more difficult for both men and women to perform acrobatic feats thus attired, but the fashions of the circus world like those of society are inexorable.

Nothing could be more incongruous than the devotion existing between our French animal trainer and his performing grizzly bear. The animal is the largest of the bear species and the most powerful and formidable, yet this owner has taught his specimen gentleness and good manners. He is its constant companion and attendant. Its long and shaggy brown coat is brushed and combed at frequent intervals, and food is proffered in bare outstretched hands. It obeys commands with all the sagacity of a well-trained dog and gives an exhibition of wrestling, pugilism and other difficult displays which interest and amuse. Its enormous paws and long sharp claws are a menace against which pads and gloves sometimes avail nothing and the foreigner is ever a sorely wounded person. Bruin has been elevated to a state of intelligence which seems to give him keen enjoyment of bear humor. Thus it is that the circus folks declare that whenever the beast slaps or hugs its human friend with unusual violence, great glee is depicted in every characteristic. No matter how the resentful trainer exerts himself, he cannot retaliate with any effect. The sight of the Frenchman chattering angrily at the unconcerned furry humorist after their performance is a weekly source of merriment in the menagerie tent.

The "rooster man" is one of the novelties of the show and of the dressing-room. He is an Englishman who costumes himself like a monstrous fighting cock, gaffed and ready for the fray, and astonishes the audience with an exhibition in which an audacious little natural game cock participates. It concludes with a battle between the pseudo and the genuine bird in which the one engages eagerly and is impressed with an exultant, strutting conviction of victory when its huge antagonist flops fluttering to the ground. The diversion is as entertaining as any in the sawdust precincts and to the show persons the most remarkable for patience in training and endurance in execution. How little the onlookers imagine that after the act the human rooster frequently drops in a state of collapse and exhaustion! The feathers which envelop him are of necessity fastened to stiff and smothering supports, and their encumbering weight on a hot day is tremendous. This is one of the secrets of the arena which probably no one who has witnessed the unique performance ever divined.

For intrepid bravery and wild exploits I doubt if the equal of the trick bicyclist can be found. In the parade, the chances of injury he gleefully assumes fill the sightseer with horror and dread. Under the canvas the greater the risk the more enjoyment it accords him. He rides, in one exhibition, down an ordinary ladder which stretches to the dome of the tent. Down the smooth rungs he dashes, like a spectral flash, and his comrades wonder what the final end will be. Nothing can prevent the feat. When wet weather makes other performers hesitate or they are directed not to try their acts, he mounts merrily to his perch and trusts to luck and skill. Water drips from the apparatus and his mad flight seems impossible of safe accomplishment. He emerges unscathed. He is, too, the dare-devil of the "cycle whirl," a cup-shaped apparatus made of wooden slats. He has four companions, but the neck-breaking scorching is delegated to him. Around the inclined track he rushes, with hands spread out and arms upraised, the contrivance shivering and rattling. Faster and yet faster he whizzes until he no longer looks like a man on a bicycle; he is a blurred line drawn around the track. Within an inch of the rim and disaster, down the drop to the very edge of the floor he rumbles with no power of guidance over his machine save his wonderful balance, and spectators catch their breath. Then a wild jump and he is bowing and smiling in the centre of the cup.

The invention of new acts engages the attention of acrobats and gymnasts most of the winter. Many of them rehearse in the gymnasiums of large cities, although aerial performers have difficulty in finding sufficiently ample quarters. They tell, in dressing-room conversation, of many queer experiences with the flabby-muscled, hollow-chested men who seek their aid and advice to attain better physical condition, and find much amusement in relating their observation of methods employed in this effort. A very rich weakling who patronizes one of the New York city gymnasiums is a never-ending source of hilarious reminiscence. He is ridiculous in all his body-building plans, but firm in his belief in their efficacy. One of his practices is to run for hours with a bag of shot tied to his head. He has persuaded himself that it will develop and strengthen his chest!

It is in the knees that the evidences of age first manifest themselves in the acrobats. The strain on this part of the body is always intense. Suddenly the veteran finds accustomed life and spring have left them. Then he knows the end of his active career has come. Many of these men, barred physically from somersaults and the like, become "understanders," that is, they are the members of troupes who catch and support their twisting comrades who alight on shoulder or ground. Their strength is still in shoulder and arm, but agility is a wistful memory.

Circus rehearsals are delayed until two or three days before the formal opening, which affords ample time for guaranteeing a smooth performance. The reason that no more preliminary time is required is due to the fact that each performer appears for the season's work perfect in his individual act. There remains only the necessity for blending into a harmonious whole. Minor details are speedily adjusted by the equestrian director. The celerity with which intelligent order is evolved from chaos is amazing to the inexperienced observer.

The pretty and pleasant and picturesque part of daily life under canvas comes after the substantial meal at five o'clock, when for two hours there is rest for all save the hard worked side-show establishment. The woman performers, busy with fancy work and sewing; the men talking over the gossip of the ring; the children playing among themselves, and with the pet ponies, form a charming picture on the greensward back of the tents. Down from the southern hills steals the softly descending darkness, swift shadows move through the lingering twilight across the big tent and hang about the lot, and color comes into the white moon above. A breeze, long desired and grateful, sweeps through the place. Naphtha torches flare as the wind blows them about. Inside the "big top," the long stretches of seats barren of spectators, the equestrian director is disciplining an obstinate "cake walking" horse; the cycle sextet perfect a new pose; the clown is acting as ringmaster, while his wife rehearses her riding act, and ten gymnasts in the high white dome of the canvas plan more breath-taking aerial flights. Suddenly the shrill shriek of a whistle, a scampering to dressing-rooms, ushers in place and the evening audience pours into the seats.

CHAPTER IX

NIGHT SCENES AND EMBARKATION

Active preparations for the departure from town begin with the setting of the sun. When the naphtha torches spread their fluttering glow and when the men in the ticket wagon lift up its end and are ready for the evening sale, then canvasman, driver and porter swarm from the comfort of hay couch or from idling group, and are ready for the night's work. Team horses feel again the weight of harness, and the march to the railroad yards is on. Horse, cook, wardrobe, blacksmith, barber and the other tents spread over the lot drop to earth, are quickly rolled up and packed away. The sound of loading stakes, chains, ropes and poles resounds through the premises. Heavy wagons are soon rumbling through the streets and left convenient to the man at the cars. Then the teamster, returning leisurely to the lot, finds his second vehicle awaiting final transfer.

Ten minutes after the performance has begun, there is a scattering of the executive force at the main tent entrance and the canvasmen take possession. The ropes and stakes holding in position the marquee and menagerie tent are loosened, and the doorkeeper moves to the open fly in the big tent, called the back door. The evening exhibition programme is arranged with the view to finishing with the trained animals as soon as possible that they may be placed safely away for the night. So it is that the elephants, camels, zebra, ponies and other led animals are off with measured tread for the cars before the show is well under way. Then cages are closed, horses hitched, side walls lowered and the caravan passes out into the night. The order "lower away!" rings sharply, and the menagerie tent drops with a heavy puff and sigh. The denuded centre poles follow it to the ground and, where a few hours before was a white encampment is now a dark, bare area, rutted with wheels, trodden by many feet and littered with peanut shells and sawdust. Only the noisy "big top," glowing like a mammoth mushroom, and the side-show canvas, where the band thumps and the "barkers" roar with tireless energy, remain to mark the spot. The work of stripping the larger tent continues throughout the performance. As fast as a performer finishes his act his appliance is deftly conveyed to a waiting wagon. The entire arena has been divested of its maze and mass of apparatus before the audience have reached the open. They stare in amazement at the changed scene, as revealed in the lights and shadows of the torches. So expeditious and so smooth has been the work of the circus men that no knowledge of the magnitude of the accomplishment was conveyed to the crowd inside. The side-show orators receive the outgoing throng with renewed clamorings. To take this last advantage and let no chance for profit escape, the tent has been kept open. The inmates yawn with the weariness and monotony of it all and eagerly await their last call to the front. Then begins a dash for the freedom and privacy which has been denied them since morning.

In the "big top" the concert band is fiddling valiantly and a woman in skirts tries to raise her voice above the noise of falling wood and stentorian command. Workmen are lugging the seats away, and tugging at ropes and stakes. The side-walls peel off as the last spectator emerges and performers hurry from their dressing-room. Then the thin white cloth roof comes tumbling from above like a monster bird; the encampment is no more. Through dark, deserted, silent streets the last man and wagon make their way. Nothing is left behind in the hurried leave taking. Everything large and small must be individually accounted for by its custodian.

PERFORMERS AT THEIR MIDDAY MEAL.

At the railroad yards the blazing torches show a picturesque, animated spectacle. Here again orderly precision prevails. The wagons are drawn on to the cars by horses and a block and tackle, while a man guides the course of the vehicle by its pole as it is passed to the far end of the car. There is a "skid" or inclined plane at the end of the first car, and an iron plate bridges the space between the other cars, making a continuous platform. Each wagon has its number and allotted place again, and is placed to the best advantage for convenience of unloading and for utilizing space. A wrongly-packed vehicle would cause endless confusion and delay. It is seldom later than one o'clock when the three sections are on the move. Rain and mud annoy and retard, sometimes, but extra efforts nullify, in a great measure, the effect of their presence. Working-man and beast are slumbering deeply when the engines couple for the journey, and only the watch-men, patrolling the long stretches of cars, give sign of life and wakefulness. At one end of the line of Pullman sleepers, where are placed the performers and members of the business staff, is the most ornate piece of rolling stock, the Thelma, named for the general manager's daughter, a tot who is eagerly awaiting her father's winter cessation from toil. Here is a queer little lunch room where gather each evening, for a bite, after the show, the men and boys of the circus. An hour or two passes with much laughter and jollity and with many innocent jokes, intermingled with serious discussion. Ice-cream is the popular dish, and plateful after plateful vanishes down dusty throats. The frozen mixture is a nightly requisite of the body-weary circus colony. It is to them what the night cap of liquor represents to the toper. No headache or clouded brain or dulled body is its concomitant, only health-giving properties. Strong drink is tabooed in the Thelma, as is its fate elsewhere with the circus, and no demand for its presence has ever been manifested. The scene is one the most approved moralist would endorse.

Hassan Ali, the giant of the side-show, is the most unwelcome visitor. Room is at a premium, and he occupies about double space. Somebody is always stepping on his protruding feet, to his intense disgust, but to the ill-concealed amusement of the others. There is a general feeling of impending disaster when Hassan is seen stooping into the room. If his huge bulk doesn't shatter a chair, his awkward movements seldom fail to break a dish, crush a by-stander or scatter food indiscriminately. Colonel Seely, the privilege man, grumbles vigorously, and none of us are at ease until the giant has retired to bed and the nightly ordeal is over. Through it all Hassan never loses his temper or composure. His good nature knows no bounds.

A veteran of the ring tells of railroad accidents and other circus disasters and reverts to the days of P. T. Barnum. "That man certainly had his troubles," he observes. "His pecuniary catastrophes and fiery ordeals would have utterly discouraged a man less stout-hearted than he. Three times his museums were burned to the ground. The number thirteen he always considered ominous, for the first of his buildings was consumed on that day of the month, while the thirteenth day of November saw the opening of the second establishment, which was likewise subsequently destroyed by fire. On July 13, 1865, while he was speaking in the Connecticut legislature at Hartford, the American Museum was consumed. Nothing remained but the smouldering debris when he arrived in New York. It had been probably the most attractive place of resort and entertainment in the United States. Here were burned up the accumulated results of many years of incessant toil in gathering from every quarter of the globe myriads of curious productions of art and nature. The indefatigable showman immediately began the erection of new buildings at Nos. 535, 537 and 539 Broadway, New York, and started a new chapter in his career. The place was levelled by flames in March, 1868, completely frustrating his plans for the future. The loss did not disturb his tranquillity and he established a "museum, menagerie and hippodrome" in Fourteenth street. Four weeks after the opening, it, too, was ablaze and no effort could prevent its total loss.

"Fire did not, either, confine its devouring presence to his professional enterprises. On December 18, 1857, his home, 'Iranistan,' at Bridgeport, became the prey of flames. His assignees sold the grounds to Elias Howe, Jr., inventor of the sewing machine, for fifty thousand dollars, which went toward satisfying the Barnum creditors, for the showman was at that time in one of his periodical financial difficulties, from which, however, he finally extricated himself. His faculty for making money always successfully asserted itself.

"I was in his employ for many years and wonder that I escaped alive. I was in a dozen crashes on the railroad, and was in Bridgeport both times the winter quarters were swept by flames. Fire first came in 1887 and destroyed the main building. The white elephant and two others, Alice and Sampson, were burned, and nearly all the other animals except a rhinoceros, one lion and a white polar bear, perished. The blaze was of incendiary origin, for the watchman told me he saw a man coming down the outside stairs of the paint shop and a few moments later was struck on the head from behind and knocked down. Immediately after, the fire burst out and illuminated the horizon for miles around. The flames spread so rapidly that the firemen could do nothing more than save the adjoining buildings, cars and wagons. The rhinoceros made his escape through a window but was so badly burned that he died. An elephant came as far as the door of the building, then turned back into the flames. Alice and Sampson also made an attempt to escape. One large lion ran out into the yard and the spectators fled in all directions. It took refuge behind a car and a policeman fired several shots into his body. This partially disabled him and a keeper succeeded in caging him. Many of the museum and menagerie curiosities were in the burned building and were destroyed. One of the engines on the way to the fire was stopped by a large elephant on the streets. There was a panic among the people and they tumbled over each other trying to get out of the way. An escaped tiger also caused a great commotion. The elephant trainer was out of town and the other keepers were unable to quiet the frightened animals. Thirty of the elephants and one large lion started across the country in the direction of Fairfield and Easton, scattering the people right and left. It was several days before they were all recaptured.

"The other fire was in 1898 when Barnum was dead and the show was in Europe. The loss was one hundred thousand dollars. We got most of the animals stored there out safely. Fifty green horses, I remember, broke from their stalls and ran mad through the streets. The townspeople were pretty frightened, for they thought some of the wild beasts were loose."

The husband of "the mother of the circus" drops in for a sandwich. His wife has retired, longing for the happiness of all and full of plans to promote it. He has been twitting the unicycle performer because the latter's wonderful feat has been made almost insignificant by comparison with the "loop-the-loop" accomplishment. The equilibrist retorts that for next season he has arranged an act that will discount anything ever seen under tent. He proposes to hoist the "cycle whirl" apparatus thirty feet from the ground and ride on its track with nothing between him and earth. There is a general protest that he hasn't the nerve or skill; but he smiles knowingly.

The discussion turns to feats of agility; it is agreed that the tight rope walker is the best tumbler with the show. The clown laments because he hasn't received the usual daily letter from the little woman he married in New York in the spring. The equestrian director tells of the circus as it used to be, and all enjoy his stories. One of the trick bicyclist's arms is in a sling; he had a bad fall during the evening performance. The family of Italian acrobats jabber tirelessly in the corner; they know nothing of our language, but their superior skill commands a big salary. A somersault rider dashes in after a sandwich for his wife, with whom he does a carrying act. The Japanese juggler and his son retire together; they are never apart. There is a laugh at the expense of the two horizontal bar performers who lost their way in the sombre village streets and were an hour in finding the car. A partial exodus begins when the word goes forth that the first section is ready to move. Those whose berths are on one of the other divisions bid good-night. So the scene and its actors shift. At midnight or soon after, the Thelma lunch-room is deserted, save for the busy porter. Dusty clothes and shoes that show inconsiderate treatment occupy his time until the yawning cook appears. Then the delicious odor of coffee pervades the quarters, and breakfast food awaits the hearty order of hungry men. They are far removed from the scene of a few hours before and gaze curiously at the surroundings. To-morrow morning the setting will be new and strange again.

CHAPTER X

THE CIRCUS DETECTIVE

To the circus organization with honest purpose the problem of dealing with the horde of "guns," "dips," "grafters" and others of their criminal ilk, who would fain be its daily companion, is perplexing and formidable. Next season the duty of protecting the person and pocket of our patrons will be a duty entrusted to new hands. Frank Smoot, for many years the circus detective, is resting a long sleep in an Illinois graveyard. A hemorrhage took his life as the circus was folding itself away for the winter. The record of his acts and his virtues will ever be inscribed upon the fleshly tablets of our hearts.

No person was ever more thoroughly equipped by nature and experience for the hidden but tremendously valuable part he played in the daily life with the circus. It was confidently averred of him that he was familiar with the figure, face and method of almost every crook in the circus world. No person of doubtful or dishonest purpose could remain for more than a few hours in company with the circus without being singled out and summarily dealt with. The treatment varied materially. Its mildness or ferocity rested entirely with the wicked one's conduct after he received the order that he take quick passage out of vision and return no more.

Mr. Smoot possessed great coolness of nerve and quickness of hand and eye. In the smaller cities his appearance at the local police station was almost simultaneous with the arrival of the circus train. He found, generally, a commander whose criminal experience had been confined to the peaceful country borders, who was entirely unaware whether or not the community had been invaded by those who would profit by the lack of worldly knowledge of the thousands of show-day visitors, and whose precautions consisted of the swearing in of numerous deputies, who wore conspicuously a bright badge of office in the happy assurance that it would permit them free entrance to the tent. But the police chief was always alive to the responsibilities of his position, offered aid, if not advice, and was ready to act when his duty was pointed out.

Then the circus detective hurried to the railroad station and scrutinized the passengers on all incoming trains. Here he sometimes found the railroad watchdog. Many of the big railroads send their detectives wherever the circus uses their lines. Their aim is to see to it that those who patronize their service do so at no financial risk. The peripatetic crook is quickly given to understand that he must use other means to travel.

The thick crowds which awaited the coming of the parade was the next scene of Mr. Smoot's activity. Here was frequently uncovered the first prey of the day, and seldom a morning passed that at least one cunning lawbreaker did not feel the weight of a heavy hand on his shoulder, and hear, sullenly, the word to march to the police station and undergo the damp solitude of a county jail cell for twenty-four hours. Then, when the circus was miles away on its course, he passed out to freedom. Where were yesterday the throng of sightseers, which had filled him with promise of great profit, were only the trodden peanut shells and the accustomed monotony of the country town. The venturesome crook who invaded the circus lot proper, was an especial object of vigilance. Sometimes Mr. Smoot stood for hours on the top of the ticket wagon, a stalwart figure outlined above the crowds, watching for his professional enemies, where he could see on every hand; again he was at the main entrance with a steady, critical survey of all who passed under the broad spread of canvas.

A promise made to him in good faith by a crook had never been broken, he used to say. I remember an interesting demonstration I witnessed of his confidence in the word of a man to whom no crime was unfamiliar. He had been discovered loitering about the grounds, and had been ordered off with a threat of immediate arrest. He resembled much a country gentleman of ample means and genial nature.

"Well, you got me quick," was his ready remark, "but seeing as I came all the way from Pittsburg and can't catch a train back until night, won't you let me see the show? I pledge you I won't do any 'business,' no matter how tempted."

His ingenuous request was granted with a feeling of security in his word by the detective, which the day showed was not misplaced.

The work of the circus detective, which calls for all his shrewdness and courage is in dealing with the dangerous, determined characters who disregard the warning to part company with the show at once, and who rejoin the organization as soon as released from a preceding day behind bars; men of plausible manners and engaging address who are ready for any desperate chance. Upon these recalcitrants swift retribution is visited. Formidable machinery which exercises a vague and terrible power is put in motion. And thus it is that the moon, rising over a country district, sometimes shines on the circus train speeding on its journey, and its clear rays stream over a deserted lot, casting strange shadows from a figure which lies as it has fallen, huddled in an ungainly heap upon the wet grass. Dawn brings animation to the form and to a hardened criminal a feeling of thanksgiving that he is still alive, and a deep conviction that hereafter his world of "graft" will be far removed from the circus and its primitive punishment.

The personality of circus men has changed materially for the better in recent years. Time was when they invariably wore high silk hats and clothes of many checks and hues. To be without diamonds on fingers and in shirt and necktie was a standing reproach to the profession. Nowadays the circus man affects little jewelry, and that unobtrusive, or none, and in his attire and speech he differs none from the man of ordinary commercial pursuits. He has established a reputation for honesty and sobriety and is an element of order and decency. He surrounds himself with associates of good character and business integrity, and cherishes highly his good standing in the community.

The increased police vigilance and protection accorded has helped to bring about this happy condition of affairs. In the past it was often necessary to save life and property by meeting the attacks of roughs and rowdies with equal violence and disorder. Circuses expected and received little or no help from supine or frightened police, and learned to fight their own battles. It has never been charged that any circus was not fully capable of meeting force with force, and the lawless affrays of the circus lot would form a bloody narrative. No show in the old days dared venture forth without a squad of picked fighters, and if the occasion demanded the whole encampment was eager and ready for the fray. The war cry "Hey Rube!" had forceful significance then. The circus man's favorite weapon was the guy stake, a shaft of wood used to support chains and ropes. An iron ring circled one end, the other was pointed enough to penetrate the hardest ground. Wielded by brawny workmen, experienced in its manipulation and skilled by long practice in the art of rough combat, the instrument mowed down the ranks of the enemy with deadly execution. Fists, knives and pistols availed nothing against the onslaught. Fear and mercy were unknown in those lawless times.

Years ago if murder was done the guilt was not always fixed upon the circus employee. The hasty concealment of a body in the hay behind the cages in the menagerie tent temporarily hid evidence of the crime. In the darkness of the departure, there was a surreptitious burial. The lifeless form was hastily conveyed under ground where had been the circus ring and where the chances of discovery and disinterment were remote. Many a victim of savage circus warfare rests in these unmarked graves, and pick and shovel would solve the mystery investing scores of circus day disappearances. Particularly in the Southern States, soon after the war, were these sanguinary battles waged and with fatal results. In justice to the circus men, let it be said that their consciences gave no reproof and they felt no sense of moral guilt for the reason that they were never the instigators of riot, that they strove to quell trouble in its incipient stages and that they fought for their lives and their employer's property. They knew, too, that public prejudice would prevent a fair legal trial and saw to it, if human ingenuity could prevail, that no serious charge could be laid against them, much less that of homicide.

CHAPTER XI

THE AUTOBIOGRAPHY OF A CIRCUS HORSE

When the circus bill posters swarmed over the farm a month ago and garnished my stable with products of their pot and brush, a shadow of sadness and melancholy oppressed me. Curiosity urged me to approach, but a sense of mortification over my ignominious fate bade me restrain myself. I kept in seclusion under a distant apple-tree and hoped to escape detection. However, I was doomed to disappointment, for soon I observed my owner, whom I detest, coming with halter and whip. Then I knew that he had revealed my identity to the showmen and they had expressed a desire to view me. At first I was disinclined to enter their presence, but the master cornered me and adjusted straps, despite my protestations. How shameful a spectacle, Tom Keene, who made for himself, at home and abroad, a place among the greatest horses in circus history, being led by a New Hampshire farmer—for the vulgar scrutiny of a group of cheap posters!

They inspected me with many evidences of interest, although I am convinced I would not have been recognized had not one of the visitors called attention to a scar on my flank and recalled the incident of a train wreck in which it was received. Then I remembered him as one of the stable men of my professional career. He called me by name and stroked me tenderly, but I was too ashamed at my position to respond to his greetings. He handed the master an order for circus seats and I felt more miserable. I knew it was inevitable that my old comrades spy me hitched to the old carry-all, along with the nags of the neighborhood, as they paraded by amid the joyous flourish of trumpets and proud and plumed. I loathed myself in the contemplation.

The succeeding days were a period of dismal foreboding. Adding to my sorrows and regret was the scarlet paper which confronted me when I entered the stable. It depicted the performance of one "Senator," a low-born pony, of whom I had a vague memory. He had displaced me with my associate of many years, Frank J. Melville. He was represented in all sorts of accomplishments, which I secretly feared were really carried out. A wave of emotion and sentiment overcame me whenever I permitted myself to gaze at the familiar figure of the man. My mind reverted to the time when he was one of the champion bareback riders and I contributed to the brilliant artistic results. How I longed to feel his slippered feet on my broad back, and hear again the plaudits of onlookers! I shall always have a warm, deep feeling for him. Perhaps, after all, he had no other recourse than to dispense with my services. I know he was much affected at the parting, and exacted a promise that I should always be given kind treatment, and that every consideration be shown my impaired leg.

Instinct told me when the hateful day was at hand. The master was up and about early and I could hear the glad shouts of the children. I had little appetite for the bountiful breakfast he spread before me, and he seemed much concerned over my want of spirit and worn appearance. I had wasted appreciably in anxiety over the ordeal before me and felt a faint sympathy for the man. I appreciated that he would feel that Mr. Melville would decide that I had not received proper care and would be angry. For myself, I was in that desperate condition of mind which is the recklessness of despair.

I was guided, to a hitching post in the main street of the town, where eager crowds awaited the arrival of the parade. We were a shabby enough outfit, the farm wagon and I, and I could summon no interest in the scene. I heard, with listless feeling, the master confide, boastfully, to all who would listen, that once I had shed great lustre upon the circus ring, and felt no humiliation when they scoffed at his words. He seemed to find great exultation in dwelling upon my former renown and my downfall, and in his present proprietorship. I caught a glimpse of several familiar faces in the throng, notably the circus detective and the commissary department man, but gave no sign of recognition. If they observed me at all, they doubtless saw nothing not in common with my neighbors from the rural districts. The crowd wondered at the tardiness of the parade, and I felt a silent contempt for their ignorance. The cages had just passed on the way to the lot and they come on the last section. The man who leads the procession passed in his carriage, inspecting and familiarizing himself with the route. I, of all the throng, alone knew him and his mission.

TEACHING HER HORSE NEW TRICKS.

Soon the faint music of the bands and the distant shriek of the calliope. The cortege was approaching. I braced myself for the trying experience. Some one shouted: "Look out for your horses! The elephants are right behind!" A policeman grabbed my bridle and I gazed at him, indulgently. I afraid! I who lived for years among them! I remembered the solemn joke of my former loved master, who used to cry, when the crowd wouldn't make way: "Keep back! A drove of loose lions are coming!" Then there had been no further pushing; everybody scampered to sidewalk or doorstep. I think it was the third uniformed horseman who recalled in me their old acquaintance. He called the attention of the rider behind, was corroborated and then the word seemed to pass instantaneously back through the parade. Some reached over and patted my sides, others spoke words of encouragement and praise, and all had a look of profound veneration. I tried to look very spruce and sprightly through it all, but candor confesses that the attempt was a feeble imitation of the old days. My blood stirred for the first time since I was in the foremost circus ranks and I lamented bitterly. Oh, for the staunch, true leg of a few years ago and Mr. Melville on my back! Again we would make all other performances appear commonplace.

The man I sought everywhere with my eyes was not in the procession and a fear possessed me that I might not be permitted to feel his hand and hear his voice. But it developed that this was farthest from my master's thought. Up to the circus grounds we progressed and I ambled to the horse tents and stopped mechanically. I was living again in former glories. Then my eyes were blessed with the appearance of my old comrade. How he kissed and hugged me and looked me over critically and asked about my welfare! And how ineffably proud and happy I was when he insisted there was never my equal in all the requirements of the ring, and there was none to say him nay! I fancied there were tears in his eyes as we hopped away toward the farm, and I gave him a last beseeching plea for a return to the old life. My three sound legs are as gifted, I'll warrant, as any four in the circus stables.

Thus was broken, for a little space, the dull tenor of my sombre life. I often assure myself that death will be brighter than the contemptuous existence I am leading. Of one thing I am convinced, the history of the circus can never be written without mentioning me, the pioneer of horses born with all the true circus instincts. I first saw the light of day in Keene, N. H., not far from the spot where I am passing my last days in oblivion. I was distinguished by a strong frame, was hardy, gentle and active, and could properly be called handsome. Mr. James A. Bailey singled me out when his circus came to New Hampshire, and my career certainly justified all the prophetic things he said about me. I was disappointed when they attached me to the pole-wagon, but felt confident that I would soon rise superior to the rather humble position. The work was long and arduous, and it was several weeks before I became accustomed to the nocturnal train rides, jammed erect among a score of other equines, but I endured it better than many of my companions. Some of them contracted a disease of the foot, caused by continued rain and mud, and in many cases it resulted fatally. I was patient and hopeful through all vicissitudes and arrived at winter quarters in physical condition that attracted general attention. Mr. Melville happened upon me soon after arrival and stopped short in admiring wonder. I knew him as a noted rider and connoisseur of horseflesh and was much elated. Next day Martin Welsh led me to new quarters. He was Mr. Melville's groom, and the delicious consciousness came that I was in their famous hands. Soon practice began as a ring animal and a great future opened before me. I meditate over the past, here in my loneliness, and wonder if mine is not a career which no other circus animal has equalled. Some of its striking features occur vividly to me.

I remember first, with pardonable pride, that it was generally conceded that I was the best "broke" horse in the history of the ring. There seemed to be a vein of harmony in the feeling existing between Mr. Melville and myself. Nothing ever made me nervous or shy. I trusted my master implicitly and I was as accurate and certain in my movements when he was turning somersaults or leaping through fire rings or balloons as when we made the preliminary canter. My broad, muscular back was ever waiting for him to alight just where he planned. Many said much of the credit for his feats was mine. Modesty prevents an expression on my part. We toured America a season and were everywhere received with warm approval. Then we set out for England. Bessie, a fine, gray horse, also from New Hampshire, accompanied us. She was a wonderfully intelligent animal, and the only horse, I understand, who ever was trained to trot in the circus ring. She used to circle the ring at a forty gait, with our owner doing all sorts of tricks upon her back. Poor girl, she died in Hamburg and I missed her sorely for years.

Our itinerary, as I recall it, was about like this: From London to Hamburg, to Russia, to Poland, to Liverpool, to France, to Holland, to France again, to Belgium, back to Hamburg, returning to London and Liverpool, once more in Hamburg and then aboard ship for our native country. Here we visited all states and territories, toured Mexico and passed on to Cuba. Ten years were consumed in our travels and nowhere did we fail to achieve emphatic success. It is a record I contemplate with a feeling of great elation, and which I have heard circus men say is entitled to unique distinction. We gave eleven private matinees before the royal family of Russia, and some of the prominent persons who witnessed our performances during our professional career were Grover Cleveland, President of the United States; the late Queen Victoria of England and her son, the present king; the Marquis of Salisbury, prime minister of England and the great leader in the House of Commons; Kaiser Wilhelm of Germany and his wife and their son, Prince Fritz; the late Prince Von Bismarck, the "man of iron;" the late Count Von Moltke, field marshal and chief of staff of the German Army, one of the world's greatest soldiers; President Carnot, of the French Republic, since assassinated; Queen Emma of Holland and her daughter, the present queen; King Leopold of Belgium; the last three Emperors of Russia, Alexander I., Alexander II., and Nicholas II; and Francis Joseph, emperor of Austria, and his accomplished wife who was later stabbed to death. What other lowly horse ever helped to enthrall the attention of such a galaxy of notables?

Many ludicrous and many sober incidents of my eventful circus life come to my mind. I was in many train wrecks. Once my car caught fire on the journey from St. Petersburg to Warsaw. There were four of us in the place and I was the only one to escape alive. Martin Welsh, my devoted friend, helped me to safety. Again, when twenty-five horses were packed in one of the circus cars in Indiana, it rolled down an embankment. I was one of five to emerge unhurt; most of the others had their necks broken. I remember, too, when I was thrown with four carloads of equine companions into the Ohio river. It happened on a Sunday run from Cairo, Ill., to Detroit, Mich. Many were drowned or perished from exposure. I floated about eight hours before being rescued and never felt any ill effects. Mr. Melville and I were on the steamer Stork which became waterlogged during the trip from Hamburg to England. We were nine days at sea, and I passed most of the time in water above my knees. I was ready for the ring when we finally landed.

I am sure that I have travelled more miles in my life than any other horse ever born and have displayed through it all more hardihood than any, save perhaps Mayfly, whose famous career has been recited many times in circus camps. He antedated me many years. They tell of his standing trip of one hundred and ninety days from Sydney, Australia, to Valparaiso, Chili, and his subsequent rough overland journey to various parts of the republic and back again to the Pacific Ocean. Then he was taken by water to San Francisco, a three months' trying experience, and later around the southern continent to New York. It was enough to wreck the finest constitution, but he never flinched. He and his sister, Black Bess, were of pure Arab extraction, and some of the finest horses in California to-day date their parentage from them. As bareback performers they have had few superiors.

Then I remember, too, many renowned animals of my time. The Russian horse Zib, who was poisoned in Mexico, achieved fame more for his tricks than his ring exhibitions. Dan Rice's horses Excelsior and Excelsior, Jr., although both blind, were wonderfully intelligent. Obeying their master's directions, they would grope to a pedestal, place the left foot on its staff, bend the right leg gracefully and incline both ears forward as if in the act of listening. How often have I, in an adjacent ring, seen the veteran clown turn proudly to the audience and heard him announce: "Mark well the beauty of the curve of the right leg, which strikes the eye of the sculptor. Horace Greeley calls them the horses with souls of men!" Levi J. North's horse Cincinnatus was probably the first "dancing" equine, and Stickney's Tammany was the best jumper that ever came to my knowledge. Wicked Will, owned by Spalding and Rogers, eclipsed most animals in difficult feats of various kinds. Rarey's horse Cruiser, although never a circus performer, was invaluable to his owner in horse "taming" exhibitions, and seemed to execute his duties with human intelligence.

Thus I live again the days of old and unfold the roll of my eventful history. My thoughts travel fondly back to the scenes I am to behold no more, and my heart throbs with emotions excited by their reminiscences. I remember those gone to their rest and shed a tear to their memory. For myself, only ignominy and mental anguish. I, who have been an honor to my birthplace and an ornament to my race, wearily await the final summons. In the array of names of illustrious circus horses, may my memory be cherished faithfully is the hope of miserable

TOM KEENE.

CHAPTER XII

THE CIRCUS BAND

BY BANDMASTER WILLIAM MERRICK

Few people who watch the circus parade as it comes down the street and who, almost invariably, cry, "Strike up the band!" "Why don't you play!" "Let her go!" etc., have ever given a thought to the amount of work that falls to the circus musician, and the experience, care and patience it requires to organize and successfully conduct this nowadays necessary adjunct to the big tent enterprises. The earlier circus bands were far from being the complete affairs of to-day, and perhaps nothing gives a more striking example of the growth in civilization and culture of our country than the evolution of the circus band.

The bands carried by the first circuses and menageries were necessarily limited in size and not always composed of the best talent. Travelling as they did by wagon, and being forced by lack of transportation facilities to curtail the number of their people, and the accommodation of the performers coming in for first consideration, the band was looked upon in those days much in the light of a disagreeable necessity. Often the engaging of the music was left to the last moment, and frequently the earlier shows were content with picking up a roving gypsy band, similar to the ones we now see playing for pennies, under the windows of the residential quarters of our large cities.

As might have been expected, the first really military bands that were introduced into the circus business were of European origin, but even they were not so complete in numbers and so especially adapted in character to the purpose as the present circus military band. Still among them were occasionally musicians of exceptional ability, and many of the better soloists of our metropolitan bands and orchestras were at one period of their career members of a travelling circus band. But it is not the intention of this article to attempt a history of all the musical notables connected with the circus, but rather to contrast the circus band of to-day with that of the past.

Let us take a glance at the repertoire of the old time circus band. The overtures and grand entree were played by brass instruments alone, the usual instrumentation being three cornets (generally two E and one B), two E horns, one B tenor, baritone and bass, the drums being played by such performers as could (to use a slang expression) "fake" a little. Two to four overtures, and perhaps one or two selections or pot-pourris, composed their entire libraries in this respect. The incidental music for the various acts was almost invariably played with string instruments, the orchestra being composed of two violins (first and second), flute or piccolo, clarionet, two cornets, trombone, and bass.

I recall an amusing incident connected with the piccolo player of one of these travelling orchestras. The leader, a very good violinist by the way, had occasion to correct the piccolo player, and asked in a very pompous manner, "Bill, why don't you play that last strain an octave higher?" To which Bill nonchalantly replied, "Professor, I am now playing higher than my salary goes." As the company was not noted for its liberality in the way of salaries, the retort was highly relished by the balance of the orchestra.

The numbers that could be produced by a small number of instruments were exceedingly few, so the libraries of the travelling leaders were of a consequence limited.

Now all this is changed. The extreme competition between the music publishers of to-day and the practicability of our experienced modern managers, render it possible for a leader who is at all enterprising to obtain not only all the standard and classical overtures and selections, but an almost endless programme of popular music for the promenade concert that now precedes the performance with every large or well regulated circus.

But to be thoroughly efficient and "up-to-date," the latter-day circus leader must not rest content with a pleasing or popular concert programme. There is the performance or incidental music to be looked after, and for this purpose the leader, to suit the varying tastes of the performers and public, must frequently draw on his own powers of composition. Every act, or series of acts, requires music exactly in keeping with its character. Nor will it do to keep one programme on too long; the performer grows tired of it, the musicians become careless, and the music itself (so fast is the age in which we live) becomes mildewed, and out of date.

By this it will be seen that the circus leader's life, if he keep abreast of the times, is a very busy one, nor is the improvement confined solely to the augmentation of the musical library. The band, instead of being confined to the poorly balanced and limited instrumentation that we have just mentioned, is composed of sufficient reed to soften the natural harshness of the brass instruments, and the individual performers are selected from the youngest and best talent our country affords. I say "youngest," for the rising generation having had the advantage of the experience and teaching of their predecessors in the "art divine," possess in a marked degree that mobility of temperament, accuracy of attack, and facility of execution, so necessary in rendering properly the circus music of the present day. Then they must begin young in the circus business to acquire the proper embouchure for playing almost an unlimited amount double forte, over rough streets, and still be able to render pianissimo in the concert programme following the parade.

No amount of practice in the conservatory or concert room can obtain this embouchure. It must be acquired by actual experience, on the circus band wagon. A band composed of the better class of musicians that have "come up" in the circus business will render almost double the volume of tone of the same number taken from the theatre orchestra or concert stage, and if they have been properly handled by a painstaking and efficient leader, the quality will be also be found superior.

The life of the circus musician, filled as it is with plenty of hard work, is not without its sunny side. The constant change of scene incident to travel alone is a great factor in dispelling weariness. The open air life renders it the most healthful of occupations, while the antics of the rustic who comes into town to see the parade and hear the band, are an endless source of amusement. The music for the parade, played as it is in a very lively tempo, causes all manner of grotesque movements among the listeners on the streets. This is particularly noticeable on the southern tours. It is no uncommon thing for a number of "darkies" to start at the circus grounds and dance through the entire route of the parade; and when in doubling back on the main street, which is often necessary in the smaller towns, the band passes the steam calliope, which brings up the rear, the din caused by the mingling of the band-music with the shrill whistle of this instrument, seems to throw them into a veritable frenzy. During one of these parades the following colloquy was overheard between two of these overexcited "darkies":

"Jim," yelled a particularly dusky individual, "look at dat man up yonda with dat slip ho'n!"

"Deuce wid de slip ho'n," replied Jim, "look at dat steam fiddle!"

I remember an astonishing but blessed effect the music of our circus band had on a woman in Grand Island, Nebraska, in 1882. She had been blind for years and was sitting dejectedly at a window as we approached in parade. When opposite her, we burst suddenly into brazen harmony, and the woman gave a scream of great joy. The shock of the music had caused her to regain her eyesight.

CHAPTER XIII

WITH THE ELEPHANTS

"Jumbo was the biggest elephant ever in this country, and few are in the secret that the tremendous success of the animal's tour was an accident of fortune," observed our elephant man. "He was an African animal and very stupid, but always good-natured. An agent of the big American circus heard that he was the tallest pachyderm in captivity and that London was anxious to sell him. The man closed the sale for two thousand pounds with no conception of the money-making prize he was securing. The beast had been a pet with the children in the London Zoological Gardens, but the announcement of his purchase by Americans was received with no especial expressions of regret. It required two weeks to build a van-like cage for the journey by sea, and then keepers went to the zoo to lead Jumbo to the ship. He strode along all right until the gate of the garden closed behind them and then lay down in the street. It was a pure case of elephantine obstinacy and the animal wouldn't budge. There he measured his length in the dust for twenty-four hours despite all urging and entreaty, to the despair of his custodians, who little realized the wonderful effect the incident would have on the owner's pocketbook.

"The English newspapers soon heard of the occurrence and promptly seized upon it for an effective 'story.' 'Dear old Jumbo,' they said, 'refused to leave the scene of his happy days with the children; his exhibition of protest was one of remarkable sagacity; they hoped he would continue to defy the Yankee showmen and remain in London; he was the pet and friend of the little ones and ought never to have been disposed of, any way.' The elephant when in repose or resistance rests on his knees, and one of the newspaper sagely remarked that Jumbo was in an attitude of prayer. The Humane Society was appealed to and someone made a sympathetic hit by telling how lonesome and melancholy was Alice, the abandoned 'wife.' The pathos of the thing was very affecting, on the surface, but a phenomenal advertisement.

"The animal finally got on his feet and marched to the boat. Weeping women and children lined the way. The circus owners were then alive to the possibilities and, concealing their identity, got out an injunction, 'in the interests of the London public,' attempting to restrain the brute's departure. Of course, it was dissolved, but it kept feeling at high pitch up to the time of sailing. I remember the Baroness Burdett-Coutts and a party of distinguished companions visited the steamer to say good-bye and left a big box of buns, of which Jumbo was very fond, for his use during the voyage.

"The story of the brute's reluctance to leave his young friends in England was judiciously spread broadcast here and he became the feature of the circus, whereas otherwise he would probably have attracted only passing attention. It was his own fortuitous conduct and not the superior skill of the showman that made his circus career so profitable. Jumbo was killed by a train at St. Thomas, Ontario, in July, 1885.

A dwarf elephant with him escaped injury, and the show made some capital by asserting that the big elephant sacrificed his own life in shielding his small companion. As a matter of fact, he was seized with another fit of unyielding stubbornness and wouldn't step down an embankment out of an express's path. He was never south of Louisville or west of Omaha. Matthew Scott was his keeper. He shared not only his bed, but his bread and tobacco with his charge. After the brute's death he followed the circus wherever it went, and during the winter visited almost daily the preserved skin and bones of his late companion.

ELEPHANT HERD "AT ATTENTION."

"There was, of course, a Jumbo II., but he was nowhere near the size of the original beast. Harnessed with electrodes and other apparatus he stood in the middle of the Stadium at the Exposition Grounds at Buffalo, N. Y., on November 9, 1901, and gave the world a practical demonstration that an elephant can take twenty-two hundred volts of electricity with apparent unconcern. If the electric current reached his nerves he manifested no sign of it. Electric wires had been run from the Exposition power house to what was to be Jumbo II.'s death platform, and when the signal was given, twenty-two hundred volts were turned on. It merely tickled the beast. Jumbo II. was unharnessed and taken back to his home in the Midway. Explanations made by the electricians were that the elephant's hide had the resistance of rubber and formed a non-conductor impervious to electricity. Others said the voltage was not sufficient. He had developed man-killing qualities, but is still alive.

"When Jumbo was brought into this country, Adam Forepaugh made great claims for his elephant Bolivar. He insisted in large type and in many newspapers and on the billboards of his route that Bolivar was bigger than the elephant from London. W. W. Cole, then conducting a show of his own, claimed, too, that his animal, Samson, was no smaller than Jumbo. Bolivar attracted great attention through the country while with Mr. Forepaugh. Finally he became so vicious that he was given away to the city of Philadelphia, where he could be more closely watched. I remember the story of the narrow escape of two lumbermen in Michigan. They came to the show very drunk and wanting to fight. They threatened Mr. Forepaugh, who stood at the door, but he said he wasn't a fighting man and sent them on into the menagerie tent. They were stalwart fellows, with muscles hardened by rough out-door work, but I doubt not the owner of the circus could have bested either one in a pugilistic encounter. Mr. Forepaugh was a man of tremendous strength and, when aroused, a match for the most skilful slugger. The boasting visitors had not been under canvas five minutes before the sound of lamentations penetrated to the door. Hurrying inside, Mr. Forepaugh found one of the men, he who had been particularly bold and aggressive and threatening, crying like a baby. Tears dropped from his eyes as he explained that he had sought out Bolivar and challenged the huge beast to personal combat. The elephant appeared to have relished the joke keenly, for he had swung his powerful trunk at the man and deftly plucked his soft felt hat from its uncombed resting place. The beast's eyes had twinkled merrily, it was averred, as he conveyed the headpiece to his capacious mouth and swallowed it at a gulp. The terrorized victim, his swagger changed to cringing fright, was too overcome to even ask for the price of a new hat as he fled toward home. Mr. Forepaugh laughed gleefully. Bolivar's digestive powers were equal to the demands of the morsel.

"Bolivar had a long and eventful history. Probably his most thrilling experience was a terrific fight with an untamed Nubian lion named Prince at circus winter quarters in Philadelphia, in December, 1885. The lion escaped from his cage, chased a keeper out of the building and proceeded to the elephant quarters. Bolivar stood nodding where he was chained to a stake near the door. Prince hesitated for a moment and then lay back on his haunches. He crept slowly forward until he was within reach of the elephant. Then he raised his paw and struck at the supine trunk. The tough skin was somewhat torn and Bolivar became instantly fully awake, and raising his trunk made a blow at the lion. The latter escaped by jumping backward, then crouched again and prepared to spring. Quick as a lightning flash was the movement which landed him on the elephant's head. But he had to deal with a power greater than his own, over which his only advantage was his agility. Bolivar easily shook him off and tossed him some distance. The contest was then quickly decided. The lion prepared for another spring. With ears flattened against his head and eyes gleaming like balls of fire he crept forward stealthily, cautiously measuring the distance. With a suppressed growl the lithe, tawny form shot through the air. The elephant's trunk was then turned over his back and his little black eyes were snapping viciously. With a motion so quick as to be almost imperceptible, the proboscis was lowered and elevated twice and then descended with terrific force, striking the lion as he was in mid-air. The beast of prey fell stunned, and before he could recover the elephant dealt him a terrific blow in the side, and reaching forward the full length of his chain he drew his antagonist toward him. Then lifting his free foot he leaned his entire weight on the fallen foe. The effect was to crush the ribs of the conquered monarch of the forest. In this manner he trampled all over the lion until life was gone. Then he raised it with his trunk, and tossed it contemptuously to the other end of the room. Bolivar sustained no serious injury in the affray. There would have been general relief among the employees if the lion had killed him, for all were in fear of their lives near the monster.

"The white elephant campaign in the '80s was about the fiercest bit of circus rivalry I was ever mixed up in," he continued. "The Barnum show was the first to get one of the brutes. Their agent bought him from King Theebaw, the erratic sovereign of Burmah. The elephant was not white, but a leprous-looking shade of flesh color. It was really the first time one of these Albinos had ever been brought out of Asia. All that the king had done in the extravagant execution of his autocratic power was as nothing compared to the sale of the white elephant, and his subjects were furious. You see, the white elephant is a sacred emblem. It is addressed as the 'Lord of Lords.' Priests prostrate themselves as it passes by and all the honors of worship are paid to it. A noble of high rank has to be its chamberlain. Its retinue is fit for a prince of the blood royal. Sickness in the sacred animal is ominous of coming evil. Its demeanor and gestures afford auguries, auspicious or sinister. For three years the Barnum white elephant made a lot of money for the show. Crowds flocked to see it, serene and placid and gently fanning itself with its wide ears, under a large Japanese parasol, native keepers meanwhile playing their queer musical instruments. It was burned to death in 1887.

"The history of the Forepaugh white elephant is more picturesque and eventful than that of the rival circus. The boss was taken all by surprise when the other show sprang the natural curiosity, but he was quick to act. Before the Barnum animal had reached this country from London, a dispatch in the newspapers from Algiers announced the purchase there by Forepaugh of a white elephant for ten thousand pounds. Its entry into America must needs have been accomplished with great secrecy and haste, for the beast was on exhibition in less than a month after the story of the sale. Then the competition for white elephant supremacy began, and it continued bitterly during the existence of the two animals. We made all sorts of charges of deceit and trickery against the Barnum elephant, and that show advertised us all over the land as cheats and impostors and swindlers. Our elephant was almost pure white. He had a car all to himself and on the way to and from the lot was swathed in cotton cloth. Only his eyes were visible and public curiosity was heightened considerably when was observed the pains we exerted to prevent a free view of the curiosity's hide. In the menagerie tent we had a performance of religious rites before the animal by reputed Burmese priests, clad in shimmering robes of yellow, red and white silk. Some observing visitor once remarked unkindly that the religious act terminated suddenly when the menagerie tent was empty and was resumed with wonderful alacrity when spectators approached. It is true that the elephant was a more snowy white on Monday than at any other time of the week, although sometimes the skin had been spotted and stained on Saturday. To prove that it was no artificial color, Forepaugh used sometimes to send the brute into the water. He was rubbed and scoured without affecting his shade. The boss was sure that there could be no charge of disguise or pretence after that, although suspicious onlookers sometimes said something about waterproof paint. Any way, we got an international authority on zoology in Philadelphia to endorse the white elephant. His sponsorship made the Barnum people furious and their circus followed us west, denouncing us everywhere. We made them madder still by buying a white monkey and making it the elephant's companion.

"In Chicago we came across an embassy from Siam which was touring this country. Forepaugh had the audacity to invite the heir-apparent to the Siamese throne, who was one of the party, to visit the show and inspect the white elephant. The royal person came, accompanied by other dignitaries, looked the beast over and muttered to the interpreter something which was apparently not complimentary. The press agent saw to it, however, that the newspapers said that the prince had declared the animal the genuine article.

"Our white elephant died from pneumonia, the newspapers told, at the winter quarters in Philadelphia. There were no details of the burial. White elephants are delicate in constitution, any way. Certain persons who thought themselves wise said that the 'dying' experience was a cessation of 'dyeing,' but they were inspired by the Barnum show. The following season a dark, natural beast, in form much resembling the white elephant appeared as 'John L. Sullivan,' the boxing elephant. He wore a glove on the end of his trunk and swung gently at 'Eph' Thompson, a colored trainer. His career as a pugilist continued for five years, when he became so big and strong that no human being could withstand his blows. He is now one of the Forepaugh herd which perform a famous dancing act.

"As a matter of fact, I know that R. F. Hamilton, the accomplished director of the Barnum & Bailey press department, has in his possession affidavits from the Forepaugh employees whose duty it was to see that the white elephant never faded, in which they confess their perfidy. A brush and snowy liquid were the only requirements."

Our circus carries a herd of twenty-five elephants and most of them are trained in all sorts of difficult elephant performances, a task requiring patience and perseverance, and a close and continuous study of the nature of each individual animal. Of all beasts, the elephant is probably the most sagacious. He never forgets. Trainers aver that after a lapse of half a century the elephant will conduct his performance as perfectly as if but twenty-four hours had gone by. Their value to a circus rests not merely upon the attraction of their ring exhibition. Their great strength makes them useful when heavy wagons defy the straining efforts of horses, and they are frequently called into other service which requires unusual power. The application of the broad head gives motion to the most obstinately stationary vehicle, and often extricates the show from annoying plight and delay.

There are two distinct species of elephants. The Asiatic differs from the African, not only in its greater size and in the characteristics of the teeth and skull, but also in the comparative small form of the ears, the pale-brown color of skin and in having four nails on the hind feet instead of three. The intelligence of the former class is greater, too, than that of the African brute, whose head is much shorter, the forehead convex and the ears of great breadth and magnitude, covering nearly a sixth of the entire body.

The average term of an elephant's life is probably about eighty years, and he is not in possession of full vigor and strength until more than thirty years old. An approximate idea of the age can be gained by the amount of turn-over of the upper edge of the ear. The edge is quite straight until the animal is eight or nine years old; then it begins to turn over. By the time the beast is thirty the edges lap over to the extent of an inch; and between this age and sixty the droop increases to two inches or more. Extravagant ideas are held as to the height of an elephant. Such a thing as an elephant measuring twelve feet at the shoulder does not exist in India or Burmah. An authority on the subject says the largest male he ever met with measured nine feet ten inches, and the tallest female eight feet five inches. The majority of elephants, however, are below eight feet, and an animal rarely reaches nine feet, the female being slightly shorter than the male. The carcass of an elephant seven feet four inches tall, weighed in portions, gave a total weight of thirty-nine hundred pounds; so an elephant weighing two tons should be common enough. The skin was about three-quarters of an inch to one inch thick.

The training of elephants for exhibition purposes is accomplished by a block and tackle and harness, so arranged as to force them into required positions. They learn easily, as compared with the cat family of animals. It is only by the most constant surveillance by the keepers, however, that the elephant is kept in good humor and not tempted to display the ferocity which is one of his natural attributes.

The first elephant ever born in captivity in this country saw the light at the winter quarters of Mr. Bailey's Show, at the corner of Ridge avenue and Twenty-third street, Philadelphia, on March 10, 1880, at twenty-five minutes to three o'clock in the morning. The event attracted a great deal of attention among scientists and students of natural history. From the time the circus went into winter quarters, several of the most distinguished physicians of the city regularly visited the prospective mother, and the diet and conduct of the animal were studied with great care. Crowds of people flocked to see the baby. Its birth disproved a great many theories which scientific men had accepted as facts of zoology since the days of Pliny. The chief of these were that the period of gestation is twenty months and twenty days, and not from twenty-two to twenty-three months as had been supposed, and that the young does not suckle the mother through the trunk but through the mouth. The baby, whose mother, Hebe, was oftener called "Baby," weighed one hundred and twenty-six pounds, was thirty inches high and measured thirty-five inches from the tip of the trunk to the crupper. It was of a pale mauve color. The trainer of Hebe explained to the scientists that the other animals in the herd were aware of Hebe's condition for months and exhibited their form of elephantine courtesy to her. Upon one occasion, he asserted, Hebe was about to fall from a broken pedestal in the ring when the other elephants rushed to the rescue. With their huge bodies they formed a cushion against which she fell, sliding gently to the ground. Whenever Hebe called, the other elephants invariably rushed to her side, and the man who tried to abuse her would have met instant death. So great was the interest aroused in the baby elephant's birth that Stuart Craven, manager of the circus, received telegrams from all parts of the United States suggesting names for her. One man offered to buy a robe for her if given a name he suggested. A lady wanted the baby called after her. The name Columbia was finally selected. After the birth of her infant, Hebe tossed the little one around like a shuttlecock, and in her frenzy twisted off a large beam with her trunk. It was found necessary to secure her with chains.

ELEPHANTS "WORKING THEIR WAY."

The next baby elephant came to life at the winter quarters of Barnum's circus at Bridgeport, Conn., at eight o'clock on the night of February 2, 1882. It was another female, and the mother was Queen, a fifteen-year-old animal. The event was expected, and at six o'clock in the evening indications of its coming were noticed. Queen was carefully chained. After fifteen minutes of laboring the baby was born. Mr. Barnum and others who were summoned did not arrive in time. The baby weighed forty-five pounds, or eighty-one less than Columbia. It was two feet six inches high and three feet long, exclusive of the trunk which was seven inches. It was perfect in form and quite strong. Its color was bluish, and it was covered with shaggy black hair an inch long. An hour after its birth it was sucking. Mr. Barnum offered fifty-two thousand dollars for an insurance on the life of the baby for fifty-two weeks. He was jubilant and said three hundred thousand dollars would be no temptation to sell her. The sire of the baby was Chief.

A woman mastering the leviathans of the animal kingdom was one of the wonders of a circus in 1887. She was Mrs. William Newman, wife of "Elephant Bill," who had grown up with the circus. She was a matronly looking person, quite stout and pleasant-mannered, devoid withal of the masculine traits that her occupation might seem to require. At her command the elephants, eight in number, marched, wheeled, countermarched, halted promptly and "grounded arms" by lying on their sides. Then, like schoolboys, delighted at a release from what they deemed duty, the huge beasts broke ranks and assumed different postures and occupations about the ring. One of them stood on his head, another turned a grind-stone with his trunk, a third walked on a revolving barrel, and several others respectively engaged, to their own apparent amusement, in dancing on a pedestal, ringing a bell and "clapping hands." Mrs. Newman gave few public exhibitions, and there has never since been a successful woman elephant trainer. For some reason, they fail in this branch of circus work, whereas in other departments they are fully the equals of the other sex.

CHAPTER XIV

THE GENERAL MANAGER

The brisk and bustling person who predominates in the stir and activity, hurry and excitement at the main entrance, is the general manager. Nothing seems to escape his watchful eye and alert ear.

He answers questions innumerable and all-embracing, settles all disputes as to admission, conveys advice, makes suggestions, gives orders, sends lieutenants all over the lot with instructions, sees to it that the crowd gets in safely but without delay, watches ticket-seller and ticket-taker, and is in general active charge of the "door."

His is a very important department of circus life, requiring peculiar natural talents, wide experience, correct knowledge of law and logic, familiarity with affairs, and ability to manipulate men and mayors. The grave responsibilities of the circus are his and they are enough to weaken brain and body.

He is one of the first men off the cars in the morning and his day frequently ends when all his comrades are sleeping with the peace and vigor perfect health and a clear conscience afford. There is no working hour when some one of his multifarious duties does not claim his attention. He is first of all a license and contract specialist. There is nothing about their force or character or price in any part of the country he has not at his finger ends. The pecuniary cost to the show of the privileges it enjoys is entirely in his keeping. His morning is devoted to municipal and county officers and office holders. His long service has made him personally acquainted with many of them in all parts of the country. He belongs to nearly all secret societies and social organizations, which helps his purposes; he distributes admission tickets with lavish freedom where they will "do good;" his instinct tells him how long to entertain and not bore, and his errand over, a favorable impression remains. The result has been the promise of gratuitous official favors and almost invariably a reduced rate for permits.

The policing of the grounds and the protection of the show and of its patrons are in the general manager's charge. In this the circus detective is his ally and adviser, but the burden of results is his. He assures the chief of police of the honest motives of the organization, tells him no thieves or criminals are tolerated, promises that there shall be no disorder or violence on the part of the circus people, and asks in return protection and cooperation. How inadequately the police of many towns can meet the needs of the occasion is told in another chapter of this book.

The circus is subject to a system of plunder, blackmail and robbery en route that is unheard of in any other business. All classes of people seem ready to render a hand in the nefarious game, considering the circus fair prey. It requires the most diplomatic management to extricate the show without financial loss or legal proceedings, and frequently, after all, it must submit to extortion to escape attachments. These are usually levied upon the ticket wagon just before the evening performance or upon a pole wagon as the tents are being pulled down. This sort of legal robbery occurs in many towns. The show may think it is getting off all right when suddenly some accident, some chance injury to property or persons, affords an excuse for a levy.

An amusing incident among the varied pretexts for "hold up" was that we encountered in Biddeford, Maine. The day had progressed without untoward incident and at nine o'clock we thought the chance of legal trouble was past. Then, suddenly, appeared an irate resident, whose home adjoined the lot, with the declaration that our monkey cage cat was his wife's, and with a demand that we return her forthwith. He may have been laboring under a truly mistaken impression, but his subsequent conduct made us believe not, for upon our decided refusal, he made an attachment. The general manager decided then to grant the visitor's claim; the feline wasn't worth legal bother and expenditure. The proceeding cost the circus nine dollars in fees and left the monkeys in mourning. It had been their playful practice to convey struggling tabby to the top of the cage and then hurl her violently to the floor.

I recall the case of a Westerner who insisted that one of our elephants had eaten his pig. Neighbors swarmed to the scene, ready with a tale of having seen the huge beast's trunk encircle the squealing victim and thrust him into a capacious mouth. The owner wanted twenty-five dollars. A canvasman, sent to investigate, found the porker under an adjacent house.

It is the solution of these and far more serious similar problems, that are a highly important branch of the general manager's work, and upon his management and disposition of them depends much money and annoyance. If the grievance is just and fair, he is ready to make ample financial reimbursement. He expects and receives imposition, but if not carried too far, he settles for cash and gets a full legal release. If the demand made is outrageous in amount, and the claimant stubborn and menacing and uncompromising, then, to his astonished dismay, he is told to carry out his threats as he sees fit. Of course, the delay of a trial or even a hearing would cost the circus thousands of dollars, but the general manager has provided against this contingency. In every town the circus exhibits, there, too, is the representative of the American Surety Company, prepared with surety for any amount. The levy is made, accepted with unconcern, financial pledge is given, and the show moves to the train and away. It is all very perplexing and painful to the man with the exaggerated sense of affliction, and he wishes he had been more moderate in speech and demand and not so hasty in action. If an amicable settlement be not made out of court, he finds that the circus will fight him to the bitter legal end.

The general manager appears like magic when there is an accident or injury in which the circus is involved. These are of almost daily occurrence. The lion or tiger may gleefully claw the too far outstretched hand of the curious boy; a horse perhaps kicks or bites; there are runaways and runovers, and a variety of other mishaps extending from cars to lot and from arrival to departure. The general manager always strives to be at the scene ahead of the artful lawyer, who would fain share in the damages. He is apologetic and regretful, offers cash remuneration and receives a written statement of satisfaction. Not until then does he breathe freely; but rest assured that in the transaction he has given no outward indication of his troubled mind and that in the bargain he has made the circus has not come out second best. The show people who watch him daily grow to look on him as ubiquitous.

Many and marvellous are the tales told him with the design of securing free admission. The street commissioner is a permanent applicant. The general manager knows the story by heart. The heavy pole wagons have damaged the highways; a few tickets will wipe out the injury. He generally gets in. The man whose land has been encroached upon by the tents; the policeman with the small army of eager children; the householder who avers the elephant's prehensile trunk mutilated an inviting tree; the alderman's brother; the clergyman who declares he has always heretofore been a welcome guest, and the long list of others with claim to recognition, get a hearing with varying success. The policeman is the most persistent. The circus is in a measure at his mercy and he is insatiable. He becomes a numerous husband and his relatives are legion. It is for the general manager to get quarter and he must go about it without offending; for there may be need for blue-coated service before the day is done, and the show must not lose official favor.

"Plain-clothes" men, the policemen assigned to duty at circus in ordinary street attire, are usually a nuisance. In the smaller towns they have little or no conception of their duties—to watch out for crooks without exciting suspicion—and they hover about the entrance, proud to be on familiar and confidential terms with the management, "passing-in" acquaintances, bothering with questions and generally obstructing the smooth progress of things. Their detective instinct and experience are nil, and their questionable value to the circus is confined to knowing the town drunkard and the tough of local notoriety, whose demeanor is sober and demure enough when opposed to the ready rank and file of the show.

Numerous special officers and sheriff's deputies have been sworn in for the occasion. These throw wide their coats, displaying to the ticket-taker their badges of office fastened to suspender or waistcoat, and are permitted to enter the tents. Their presence is needed, the general manager has been gravely assured, to aid in the police arrangements in the contingency of riot or panic. The circus knows, of course, that they are the friends and relatives of the official heads of the town, who manage, with the immunity from payment the badge conveys, to see the show free. In case of trouble or a call for their services not one of them would respond.

When the general manager is in a facetious mood and has an idle moment, we have a stock joke ready for the "plain clothes" arrayed at the door. I bustle up to the ropes, throw open my coat as if revealing a hidden badge of office; the doortender, who enjoys the diversion immensely, nods assent and I pass in. Then the stolid wits of the detectives operate and they move in a body to the serious-visaged manager and whisper that he has been imposed upon, that I am a stranger and not a special officer as I represented, and therefore not entitled to admission. My friend waxes very indignant, I, agitated and crestfallen, am led back to the entrance, lectured sternly and threatened with arrest as an impostor, and ejected. The detective force, glutted with pride over the masterly accomplishment, receives profuse thanks. Later the manager and I have a hearty laugh together.

The canvasmen and teamsters, hearty, brawny fellows, and peaceable unless inflamed with liquor, all respect and esteem the manager and appreciate that, while he is unrelentingly severe when there is an infraction of rules, his discipline is always fair and impartial. He plays no favorites. For profanity and vulgarity he will accept no mitigating excuse. In Johnstown, Pa., we were walking to the lot one beautiful Sunday morning when the loud oaths of a driver attracted our attention. He was directing his foul expressions at a child, who in its curiosity to see the gorgeous wagon, had narrowly escaped being run over. Residents, sitting at windows or on piazzas, were shocked at the vile outpouring. They had never before appreciated the resources of the language.

"Come down off the seat!" sternly commanded the manager, his face grim and hard with anger. "Now, go get your pay. You are discharged."

Then he mounted the red and gilded heights of the vehicle, clucked to the eight horses and drove like a veteran to the show grounds. The staff detective was instructed to see to it that the culprit was not permitted on the lot.

We showed two days in Pittsburg and there was afforded an opportunity to witness the wealth of resource, the courage, the tactful skill and the untiring energy of the man. All went smoothly and serenely the first day. Then came Saturday, when the workmen of the circus received their weekly pay. Across the street from the tents was a combined saloon and hotel, which at once became the focus of dissipation. A wave of inebriety seemed to sweep in upon teamsters and canvasmen. One by one they became extremely drunk and reduced new-found friends to the same condition. By night all order and decency had been abandoned and they stood about the bar or lot shouting and swearing, and making threats with knives or clubs. The season was just beginning and time had been too short for a discovery and weeding out of the tough characters among the help. The owner was making a hurried visit to his home, three hundred miles distant, and the general manager met the critical situation alone. How he managed to conduct the performance, to break camp with the few employees who remained staunch and true, and to load the trains and move out of the city, none of our feeble brains could ever grasp. But he accomplished it without serious delay, without an affray of consequence, and with a finish and skill which veiled from the public the fact that anything out of the usual was happening. Before the start from the railroad yard there was a careful and systematic count of men, stock, wagons, baggage and apparatus, for some of the drivers, continuing the debauch, had deserted their horses and vehicles in front of saloons. All were finally rounded up. The transgression cost seventy-five men their positions, and for the rest of the season other circuses marvelled at our state of grace and piety.

The general manager is rich in worldly possessions and free with cash and credit. When one's supply of money runs short, from "butcher" to man of high rank, he turns for temporary relief to his more fortunate and more provident comrade. His wants are always supplied, except in isolated instances, for not to pay a just debt entails the blight of universal condemnation and loss of confidence and honor. It is in winter, when the general manager is hiding from mankind in a Florida shelter, that the demands come fast and urgent and never pass unheeded. For then it is that the thriftless circus man, who knows no business except that which warm weather provides, is in a pecuniary predicament. The manager's bounty extends to his friends in all parts of the country, but a few weeks of the next season sees it returned to him with grateful appreciation.

CHAPTER XV

AMERICAN CIRCUS TRIUMPHANT

OFFICIAL ROUTE
CIRCUS
[SAMPLE ITINERARY]

DATE	TOWN	STATE	RAILROAD	MILES
Apr. 2-19	New York	N. Y.		
	Sunday			
" 21-26	Philadelphia	Penn.	Penn. R. R.	99
	Sunday			
" 28-29	Baltimore	Md.	"	113
" 30	}			
May 1	} Washington	D. C.	"	50
" 2	Hagerstown	Md.	B. & O. R. R.	77
" 3	Cumberland	"	"	124
	Sunday			
" 5	Clarksburg	W. Va.	"	124
" 6	Fairmount	"	"	32
" 7	Connellsville	Penn.	"	70
" 8	Washington	"	"	96
" 9-10	Pittsburg	"	"	42
	Sunday			
" 12	Johnstown	"	Penn. R. R.	79
" 13	Altoona	"	"	39
" 14	Lewistown	"	"	75
" 15	York	"	"	97
" 16	Reading	"	"	89
" 17	Pottsville	"	"	36
	Sunday			
" 19	Wilkesbarre	"	"	118
" 20	Scranton	"	C. R. R. of N. J.	18

DATE	TOWN	STATE	RAILROAD	MILES
" 21	Allentown	Penn.	C. R. R. of N. J	103
" 22	Easton	"	"	17
" 23	Elizabeth	N. J.	"	62
" 24	Jersey City	"	Penn. R. R.	14
	Sunday			
" 26-31	Brooklyn	N. Y.	Ferry	
June 2	Paterson	N. J.	Erie R. R.	17
" 3	Newburg	N. Y.	"	47
" 4	Kingston	"	West Shore	32
" 5	Schenectady	"	"	70
" 6	Gloversville	"	W. S. F. J. & G.	37
" 7	Utica	"	N. Y. C. & H. R.	61
	Sunday			
" 9	Poughkeepsie	"	N. Y. C & H. R.	165
" 10	Danbury	Conn.	N. Y. N. H. & H.	63
" 11	Ansonia	"	"	30
" 12	Meriden	"	"	31
" 13	Holyoke	Mass.	N.Y.N.H.&H.-B.&M.	49
" 14	Greenfield	"	B. & M.	38
	Sunday	"		
" 16	Gardner	"	"	40
" 17	Lowell	"	"	13
" 18	Lawrence	"	"	13
" 19	Concord	N. H.	"	45
" 20	Manchester	"	"	18
" 21	Haverhill	Mass.	"	33
	Sunday		"	
" 23	Portsmouth	N. H.	"	33
" 24	Biddeford	Me.	"	43
" 25	Portland	"	"	15
" 26	Lewiston	"	Grand Trunk	35
" 27	Berlin	N. H.	"	74
" 28	Sherbrooke	Quebec	"	99
	Sunday			

105

DATE	TOWN	STATE	RAILROAD	MILES
June 30	Montreal	Quebec	C. P.	102
July 1	"	"	"	
" 2	Valleyfield	"	C. P. & C. A.	
" 3	Ottawa	Ont.	C. A.	52
" 4	Cornwall	"	N. Y. & O.	85
" 5	Kingston	"	Grand Trunk	57
	Sunday			
" 7	Belleville	"	"	51
" 8	Peterboro	"	"	64
" 9	Barrie	"	"	88
" 10	Toronto	"	"	64
" 11	Hamilton	"	"	39
" 12	Brantford	"	"	27
	Sunday			
" 14	Guelph	"	"	36
" 15	Stratford	"	"	40
" 16	Woodstock	"	"	23
" 17	London	"	"	29
" 18	St. Thomas	"	L. E. & D. R.	15
" 19	Chatham	"	Grand Trunk	62
	Sunday			
" 21	Buffalo	N. Y.	"	186
" 22	Rochester	"	N. Y. C. & H. R.	69
" 23	Geneva	"	"	51
" 24	Auburn	"	"	26
" 25	Cortland	"	Lehigh V'y	43
" 26	Binghamton	"	D. L. & W.	43
	Sunday			
" 28	Ithaca	"	"	55
" 29	Elmira	"	"	70
" 30	Williamsport	Penn.	Penn. Line	78
" 31	Lock Haven	"	"	25
Aug. 1	Dubois	"	"	101
" 2	Butler	"	"	122

DATE	TOWN	STATE	RAILROAD	MILES
	Sunday			
Aug. 4	Wheeling	W. Va.	B. & O.	110
" 5	Zanesville	Ohio	"	83
" 6	Mansfield	"	"	87
" 7	Lima	"	P. Ft. W. & C.	86
" 8	Springfield	"	D. S.	67
" 9	Columbus	"	Big Four	45
	Sunday			
" 11	Piqua	"	P. C. C. & St. L.	73
" 12	Richmond	Ind.	"	47
" 13	Indianapolis	"	"	68
" 14	Anderson	"	Big Four	36
" 15	Marion	"	"	33
" 16	Logansport	"	P. C. C. & St. L.	40
	Sunday			
" 18	Springfield	Ill.	Wabash	195
" 19	Jacksonville	"	"	34
" 20	Quincy	"	"	87
" 21	Keokuk	Iowa	Burlington	43
" 22	Burlington	"	"	43
" 23	Galesburg	Ill.	"	40
	Sunday			
" 25	Kewanee	"	"	32
" 26	Sterling	"	"	92
" 27	Aurora	"	C. & N. W.	70
" 28	Elgin	"	"	27
" 29	Racine	Wis.	"	72
" 30	Waukesha	"	"	42
	Sunday			
Sept. 1	Marinette	"	"	205
" 2	Green Bay	"	"	52
" 3	Oshkosh	"	"	48
" 4	Janesville	"	"	103
" 5	Freeport	"	C. M. & S. P.	50

DATE	TOWN	STATE	RAILROAD	MILES
Sept. 6	Rock Island	Ill.	C. M. & S. P.	93
	Sunday			
" 8	Peoria	"	C. R. I. & P.	100
" 9	Lincoln	"	C. & A.	93
" 10	Pontiac	"	"	64
" 11	Bloomington	"	"	35
" 12	Danville	"	Big Four	80
" 13	Lafayette	Ind.	Wabash	47
	Sunday			
" 15	Huntington	"	"	84
" 16	Defiance	Ohio	"	84
" 17	Toledo	"	"	29
" 18	Findlay	"	T. & O. C.	44
" 19	Bellefontaine	"	Big Four.	63
" 20	Dayton	"	"	58
	Sunday			
" 22	Chillicothe	"	C. H. & D.	81
" 23	Athens	"	B. & O. S. W.	60
" 24	Charleston	W. Va.	T. & O. C.	103
" 25	Huntington	"	C. & O.	50
" 26	Mt. Sterling	Ky.	"	107
" 27	Lexington	"	"	33
	Sunday			
" 29	Chattanooga	Tenn.	I. & C.	254
" 30	Tullahoma	"	N. C. & St. L.	82
Oct. 1	Nashville	"	"	69
" 2	Paris	"	"	117
" 3	Jackson	"	"	80
" 4	Memphis	"	"	85
	Sunday			
" 6	Tupelo	Miss.	K. C. S. F. & M.	105
" 7	Birmingham	Ala.	"	146
" 8	Anniston	"	Southern	64
" 9	Rome	Georgia	"	62

DATE	TOWN	STATE	RAILROAD	MILES
Oct. 10	Atlanta	Georgia	Southern	74
" 11	Athens	"	S. A. L.	73
	Sunday			
" 13	Augusta	"	S. A. L.-C. & W. C.	119
" 14	Anderson	S. C.	C. & W. C.	103
" 15	Greenwood	"	C. & W. C.-S. A. L.	63
" 16	Greenville	"	Southern	59
" 17	Spartanburg	"	"	32
" 18	Charlotte	N. C.	"	70
	Sunday			
" 20	Wilmington	"	S. A. L.	187
" 21	Florence	"	A. C. L.	110
" 22	Columbia	"	"	82
" 23	Sumter	"	"	43
" 24	Charleston	"	"	94
" 25	Savannah	Georgia	"	115
	Sunday			
" 27	Jacksonville	Florida	A. C. L.	172
" 28	Waycross	Georgia	"	75
" 29	Valdosta	"	"	59
" 30	Thomasville	"	"	45
" 31	Albany	"	"	58
Nov. 1	Americus	"	C. of G.	36
	Sunday			
" 3	Macon	"	"	70
" 4	Columbus	"	"	100
" 5	Montgomery	Ala.	"	95
" 6	Selma	"	W. of Ala.	50
" 7	Meridian	Miss.	M. & O.	73
" 8	West Point	"	Ill. Ct. Y. & M. V.	9
	Sunday			
" 10	Kosciusko	"	Y. & M. V.	70
" 11	Greenwood	"	"	73
" 12	Greenville	"	"	132

DATE	TOWN	STATE	RAILROAD	MILES
" 13	Vicksburg	Miss.	Y. & M. V.	82
" 14	Ft. Gibson	"	"	30
" 15	Baton Rouge	La.	"	116
	Sunday			
" 17	New Orleans	"	"	89
" 18	"	"	"	
" 19	"	"	"	

Home Sweet Home 1,015 miles via I. C., B. & O., S. & W., and B. & O. R. R.

Summary:
Number of miles travelled,   11,569.
Number of States and Provinces visited,   26.
Number of towns visited,   167.

TRANSFERRING FROM WATER TO RAIL.

The conquest of the Old World by the Barnum & Bailey circus will live forever in the stirring history of tented organizations. It made the enterprise an object of international interest. There is now practically no country in the world that does not know the Barnum & Bailey Show and recognize that it and its ally, the Forepaugh & Sells Brothers Show, enjoy a happy, undisputed monopoly.

As America reaches out for commercial predominance, so the American circus challenged competition abroad, and foreign rivals quivered and shrunk. England found and felt herself laboriously behind hand, and other nations yielded pre-eminence. For five years crowned heads showed gracious appreciation and vied with one another to express generous sentiments of welcome and appreciation to the American envoy, and that period records uniform success and not a single failure. This profound impression made in other lands is one of the proudest achievements of American sagacity, resolution and ambition, and directly stimulating to the pride of all Americans, whose great good fortune it is now that the Barnum & Bailey circus has returned to contribute to the happiness of humanity here.

Few, probably, appreciate the tremendous undertaking involved in this picturesque invasion, and the difficulties met and overcome. All methods had to be adjusted to new surroundings and new demands. The manner and matter of work bore no resemblance to those here. The extent and nature of changes affected all departments of the organization. Every inch of the territory travelled was unfamiliar. Languages and people were strange. Yet the campaign was instituted without prolonged preparation and with no twinges of misgivings, so accustomed was this great circus to demonstrating possibilities and so perfect was it in planning and directing. It can truly be said that it caters for the world.

A volume in itself would be required to tell the story of how the Barnum & Bailey circus, in the stern test of competition, forced all others into insignificance during its travels abroad. Incidents grave and gay, of life, action and adventure, crowd the history of those five years. The then Prince of Wales, now King Edward VII., I recall, after witnessing several performances, sent the personal message: "The circus is justly deserving of the title 'The Greatest Show on Earth', for it not only is certainly the greatest amusement enterprise ever organized, but also the most wonderful example of organization and discipline one can hope to see."

Even more signal an honor was that conferred by Emperor Francis Joseph I., during the visit of the circus to Vienna. Following an afternoon under tents, his delighted imperial majesty sent to Mr. James A. Bailey, managing director, accompanying a letter of thanks for his entertainment, a gold cigar case, relieved on one side by the royal crown and the initials "F. J. I." Twenty-five scattered brilliants enhanced the intrinsic value of the gift. Later the royal household requested a complete set of circus lithographs for the Emperor's library.

The transportation of the show from London to Hamburg is noteworthy from the fact that it was the first time railway cars sixty feet long had ever been loaded on board ship without being taken apart. And they were taken from the vessel and deposited on the tracks in Germany just as they were removed from the tracks in London, wheels and all, and were the first English-made cars ever operated in the Kaiser's domain. The Barnum & Bailey circus was the first tented institution allowed to spread a canvas in Berlin. After a rigid examination of the show in every detail, the officials signed permits with the frank expression that they had no apprehensions of disaster in any form. The city is the headquarters of the German army, and the discipline, precision and business common-sense of the circus civilians so impressed the principal officers that they were in constant attendance. On the evening of departure members of the General Staff witnessed the breaking of the encampment, taking copious notes, while another body put in the night at the scene of embarkation at the railroad yards.

Tributes like these to the enterprise and energy and superior skill of the American circus men covered the almost continuous period of their foreign wanderings. Of difficulties overcome, there was one whose extraordinary character I feel certain would have caused any other than Mr. James A. Bailey, the director of the Barnum & Bailey circus, to have abandoned the project entirely. A few days before the opening of the show in the Olympia in London, the County Council decided that more precautionary fire measures were necessary, and ordered the erection of a giant curtain of iron and asbestos, to cover one entire side of the vast amphitheatre. The required outlay was $90,000, but Mr. Bailey, not a bit dismayed, went at the task with characteristic vigor and without delay, and accomplished it with a celerity which filled the English mind with astonished wonder. Moreover, when it came to hanging the tremendous area and the workmen in the employ of the firm to whom the contract had been given feared to go aloft, he called his own picked body of employees to the scene and they did the job without friction or flinching.

I can truly say that no one is more honored in circus history than Mr. Bailey, the presiding head of this remarkable institution. It would be a grateful duty to the world to rescue from self-imposed oblivion the events connected with his life, but the unusual modesty of the man forbids. While others boast and glorify themselves, the admitted "king of circus men" chooses personal obscurity. All publicity attaching to his movements is strangely distasteful; he wants the world to know and approve only the enterprise to which his life has been devoted and which his sagacious efforts have solely borne to supremacy. No imagination save his was once bold and radical enough to grasp the future, and no other prophet could foretell the rapid and enormous development of the American circus.

Only his old-time intimate associates know how visionary were once accounted the broad methods which have won him success, and the rebuffs and hindrances of no common sort which were his experiences. Through them all he worked ceaselessly, patiently, resolutely, with the courage and confidence of personal conviction, resigning personal convenience, ease, social enjoyment and other valued privileges, and the result has marked him as the one dazzling genius of the profession. To his employees he is like a father who sympathizes with his children in their varied circumstances of joy and sorrow. His benevolences are large-hearted but judicious, and his integrity of the rugged, old-fashioned type. He has shed a lustre upon the profession which has won universal recognition and admiration, and little wonder that his return to his native land, his rightful circus heritage, has been hailed with a burst of cordial welcome and enthusiasm.

CHAPTER XVI

THE OLD-FASHIONED CIRCUS

"The size of the tent was rather staggering at first, as the greatest length of the oval is nearly two hundred feet, and standing at one end it is impossible to distinguish with the naked eye the features of those on the crowded seats at the other end."

I quote the foregoing paragraph, taken from a newspaper of 1877, as illustrating by comparison the physical magnitude of the circus of to-day. Our "big tent" could stow away in its capacious depths half a dozen of the canvas arenas of twenty-five years ago, and our "menagerie top" covers more area. The scanty side-show cloth, an insignificant detail of the encampment, is not much smaller.

Is the modern circus, with its bewildering array of man and beast marvels, an improvement from the public standpoint over the old-fashioned show wherein the clown predominated and one ring sufficed? Has there come with the expansion more skill and hazard of performance? Do patrons relish the relegation to oblivion of some time-honored circus accomplishments, and the interpolation of vaudeville? The circus performer of former days will invariably answer these interrogations in the negative; the circus owner and manager makes no hesitation in disagreeing on all points, and his conviction is that backed by the weight of ticket wagon receipts. Whatever the artistic merits and the drifting away from things traditionary, certainly the opportunities for profit have multiplied with the years. Everything favorable, there is no more wonderful a money-maker than the modern circus. Despite frequently expressed longing, it is not likely that the public would receive with favor the return of the old-fashioned circus, no matter how alluring the performance in its meagerness. The case of the small circus of to-day bears this out. It is ignored if a "big show" is headed its way.

After retrospective talks with many old performers I cannot discover that the modern generation of athletes has kept pace with the progress of the business department of the circus. There are few legitimate circus feats executed nowadays, so far as I have been able to learn, which were not equalled in years gone by, and there are instances where supremacy is yielded to the men now retired; many of their accomplishments have not been duplicated. I cite the case of George Bachelor, who was accustomed to single somersault over ten elephants, and of "Bob" Stickney, who without apparent exertion turned two somersaults in his flight over twenty-three horses. Oscar Lowanda has been the only person to improve materially upon former equestrian acts. He succeeds in doing a back somersault from the haunch of one moving horse to that of another. In aerial performances few new individual feats are in evidence. The strides forward seem solely in the employment of more persons in a single act. The Potters perform ten in number, an unheard-of achievement a few years ago. The strain of planning and successfully carrying out the act, however, is so intense that the head of the troupe had decided to partially disband it when I talked with him.

The life of the circus man of to-day is a continual round of ease and luxury as compared with the strenuous, haphazard existence of his brother of a few decades ago. The memory of this generation can shed no light on the origin of the circus in this country, and there is no literature definitely disclosing when the first travelling organization reared its canvas. Seth B. Howe was the first circus owner of note. "Bob" Stickney, still a vigorous reminder of former days, remembers the stories told of that time by his father, Samuel Peck Stickney, who was a member of the company. The advance agent made his lonely journey on horseback. His saddle-bags bulged with circus "paper," which he tacked wherever his judgment suggested, for it comprised a welcome addition to the community's supply of reading matter. He was a smooth-tongued, polished man of the times and full of wonderful tales of the approaching circus. Curiosity and excitement were at high pitch when the caravan put in its appearance a fortnight later. The line halted on the outskirts of the town, uniforms were donned and a parade made to the scene of exhibition. This was frequently in the spacious yard of the local tavern. The centre pole of the tent was cut daily in the abounding woods, trimmed and dragged into place. The tavern provided chairs and the church was drawn upon for benches. An extra charge was imposed for the use of these resting places. Admission to the circus carried with it only the privilege of viewing the performance standing. At night, candles furnished illumination.

Trained horses and ponies composed much of the show. The feats of the equestrian were amazing in their daring, to the onlookers of that period. The ringmaster made a preliminary announcement. The rider, he proclaimed, would stand erect on a horse in full motion! This accomplished, amid wild enthusiasm, the hero of the hour balanced himself on one foot and concluded by playing a violin as the horse cantered around the ring. This was before the broad saddle pad had gone out of circus use. The rider who first jumped over banners was given a fabulous salary, and he who dared plunge through the familiar paper balloon became rich in a year.

The night overland journeys of these old-time circuses were full of dire peril. Highways were dark and dreary and places of pitfalls. Each circus wagon bore a flickering candle torch, showing the route to the driver behind. Soon menageries were added, and then an elephant. Hannibal, the "war elephant," was one of the first. There were few nights when his services were not required to extricate a wagon from mud or gully, or to urge it up some steep incline. The old Van Amburg circus transported a giraffe, a mournful beast which few modern circuses are possessed of. Wood choppers went ahead to clear the road with their axes and permit the passage of the high cage. Then came, in order of time, the side-show, with the free exhibition in front—wire-walking, a balloon ascension, a high-diving performance, or feats on the "flying" trapeze.

Probably the most noted knight of the sawdust ring was Dan Rice, who died in Long Branch, N. J., on February 22, 1900, at the age of seventy-seven years. His history was practically that of the circus—the real old-fashioned circus—in America. Daniel McLaren, his father, nicknamed him Dan Rice, after a famous clown he had known in Ireland, and the name clung to him. He touched the heights and depths of circus luck, making in his life three independent fortunes and losing one after another. He died comparatively poor. As acrobat and later clown, he travelled every portion of the United States and extensively in Europe. He first appeared as a clown in Galena, Ill., the home of U. S. Grant, in 1844, and from that time his popularity as a circus clown increased amazingly. He retired in 1882, a hale old man of sturdy frame and resonant voice, whose hearty handshake it was a pleasure to feel.

Bobby Williams, Sam Lathrop, Sam Long, Joe Pentland, Billy Kennedy, Jimmy Reynolds, William Wallett, Frank Brown, Nat Austin, Herbert Williams, Dan Gardiner, Bill Worrell and Tony Pastor were other noted clowns and "Shakespearian jesters" of his day, and most of them are hale and hearty to this day. A press agent of their time, not behind his lavish-languaged modern brother, called attention to this group as "jolly, jovial representatives of Momus, whose fund of wit and humor has given them the proud titles of America's greatest wits and punsters; scholarly, refined and every one fit to grace the proudest court as its greatest jester. Merrier men within the limits becoming mirth live not upon man's footstool—this greatest earth."

HUMILIATION OF THE KING OF BEASTS.

In the old days of the clown, when one ring furnished satisfying enjoyment, his was a very important and conspicuous part of the performance. His efforts of entertainment occupied the sole attention of the audience at times, as with voice or action he provided fun and folly. It was as a songster that he was at his best. Perched on a stool in the centre of the ring—thrown up of soil and not the portable wooden, forty-two foot diametered affair of to-day—his vocal enlivenments were a source of much laughter and merriment. Here is a type of the old-time clown song, which none who ever witnessed one of the shows will fail to recall:

> I don't mind telling you,
>   I took my girl to Kew,
> And Emma was the darling creature's name.
>   While standing on the pier,
> Some folks did at her leer,
>   And one and all around her did exclaim:
>   Whoa, Emma! Whoa, Emma!
>   Emma, you put me in quite a dilemma.
>   Oh, Emma! Whoa, Emma!
> That's what I hear from Putney to Kew.
>
> I asked them "what they meant?"
>   When some one at me sent
> An egg, which nearly struck me in the eye.
>   The girl began to scream,
> Saying, "Fred, what does this mean?"
>   I asked again, and this was their reply:
>   Whoa, Emma! etc.
>
> I thought they'd never cease,
>   So shouted out "Police!"
> And when he came he looked at me so sly
>   The crowd they then me chaffed,
> And said "I must be daft,"
>   And once again they all commenced to cry:
>   Whoa, Emma! etc.
>
> An old man said to me,
>   "Why, young man, can't you see
> The joke?" And I looked at him with surprise.
>   He said, "Don't be put out,
> It's a saying got about,"
>   And then their voices seemed to rend the skies:
>   Whoa, Emma! etc.

After a round of jokes and other buffoonery at the expense of the ringmaster, who retorted with threatening crackings of whip, he was ready with more melody. Sometimes he appealed to the tender emotions. "Baby Mine" was a favorite. It ran thus:

> I've a letter from thy sire,
>   Baby mine, Baby mine;
> I could read and never tire,
>   Baby mine;
> He is sailing o'er the sea,
> He is coming back to me,
> He is coming back to me,
>   Baby mine, baby mine;
> He is coming back to me,
>   Baby mine.
>
> Oh, I long to see his face,
>   Baby mine, Baby mine;
> In his old accustomed place,
>   Baby mine;
> Like the rose of May in bloom,
> Like a star amid the gloom,
> Like the sunshine in the room,
>   Baby mine, Baby mine;
> Like the sunshine in the room,
>   Baby mine.
>
> I'm so glad I cannot sleep,
>   Baby mine, Baby mine;
> I'm so happy I could weep,
>   Baby mine;
> He is sailing o'er the sea,
> He is coming back to me,
> He is coming back to thee,
>   Baby mine, Baby mine;
> He is coming back to thee,
>   Baby mine.

The clowns of the modern circus must needs possess, they confidently assert, more vivacity, wit and observation than their predecessors. The magnitude of the spread of canvas almost entirely precludes the possibility of effective oral utterance, and their drollery is confined to gesture, movement and posturing. This dumb acting places the funmaker at a decided disadvantage, and the problem of creations that will meet public favor is one requiring unusual natural aptitude. Frank Oakley ("Slivers"), fitted by nature for the part, sprang into wonderful public favor in a season.

In the grateful shade of the "big top," during the period between the two performances, I sat one afternoon with an old-time performer whose age keeps him from the ring, but the memory of whose famous feats retains him in the employ of the circus. The seductive fascination and charm of the life has never dulled within him, and until accumulated years finally forbid, he declares he will be a member of the organization. He was in a reminiscent mood and began:

"In the old days I remember a feature of our circus was Nettie Collins's lilt 'Dance me on Your Knee.' The band played the flowing melody, and she bowed and waved as she sang on a little platform in the ring. It made a great hit for several seasons. Here's how its lines went, and many an old-time circus goer will call them to mind:

When I was a little girl and full of childish joys
I used to play with all the girls, but oftener with the boys;
And with them climb the apple trees, and races, too, we'd run,
I'll tell you, oh, 'twas then, my boys, we had such jolly fun;
But now those days are past and gone, no more them I will see,
If I could only call them back, how happy I would be.
  You may dance me, darling, dance me,
  You may dance me on your knee.
  If there's such a man among you
  As can recommend himself to me,
  Be sure he's brave and strong enough
  To dance me on his knee.

"Then 'Dick' Turner, comedian, in bucolic attire, would stand up in a conspicuous place in the reserved seats, gesticulate emphatically and shout: 'I'll dance you on my knee, girl.' Most of the audience would be deceived as to his identity, supposing him to be a rural visitor to the show, and there was great hilarity. 'Come down here, then,' the ringmaster would respond, and amid shrieks of laughter 'Dick' would make his way to the ring, where the fun continued. Oh, it was easy to entertain in those simple old days!

"'Al' Meaco was a favorite with his songs and jokes. He was one of the first general clowns, and did a drunken act on stilts that convulsed the house, but was a hazardous performance, withal. One of his idiotic stories which afforded great amusement in the country districts was: 'I've got a beautiful girl. Went to see her the other night. Met her on the woodshed. Oh, the tears I would shed for her and the tears she would shed for me would be shed more than the wood shed would shed for me.' Then he did some fancy steps, the band played and everybody laughed. What a ghastly proceeding with the modern circus!

"'Al' did an act with his brother 'Tom' which was considered a marvel then. 'Al' swung head down from a trapeze, attached his teeth to a strap which belted his brother and whirled him in circles. The act is an old one now and vastly improved upon. I remember once 'Al' forgot himself, opened his mouth to speak to 'Tom' and the latter revolved forty feet through the air to the earth below. He broke four ribs and a collar bone.

"Here's another joke which one of our clowns got off with success. Nowadays it would be received with grief and shame. 'I had a girl named Sal Skinner. I called at her house one Sunday. She wasn't home. Her mother said she'd gone to church. I started out looking for her. Went into the church and walked down the aisle, but didn't see her. The minister spotted me. "Are you looking for salvation?" he says. "No," I says, "but I'm looking for Sal Skinner."' The audience howled with mirth.

"Sam Lathrop used to make mock political speeches, with flings at the politicians in the town we were playing. The best received of his assortment of jests was this one, given as the ring horse halted: 'Well, you stop, the horse stops, the music stops, I stop, but there's one thing nobody can stop.'

"'What is the one thing nobody can stop?' followed the ringmaster.

"'Why, a woman's tongue!'

"The ringmaster, in apparent retaliatory discomfiture, would crack his whip at the legs of the clown, who uttered 'Ouch!' as if in pain, and the onlookers thought it all very funny.

"Trained animals formed an important feature of our programme, and we gave exhibitions which have not been repeated since. One of our men drove a troupe of buffaloes in tandem line around the ring. 'Grizzly' Adams had performing bears, a dozen of them, and never was greater courage required. Dick Sands put a herd of camels through tricks and raced with a hippopotamus. Dan Costello showed the full-blooded Spanish bull, Don Juan; and John Hagenbeck taught a company of zebras difficult paces. George Arstinstahl, I think, was the first to group different animals. He bunched elephants, bears, lions, tigers and dogs before astonished audiences without ever a suspicion of fight."

Three noted old-time circus riders, whose fame was world-wide a few years ago, are members of our organization this season, assisting the management. They are "Bob" Stickney, whose equestrian and acrobatic feats are still fresh in the minds of all circus goers, and Frank J. Melville and William E. Gorman, who were comfortable on any part of a horse's body, barring, perhaps, the ears. They will live forever in the annals of the circus. Timothy Turner was the first to somersault on a horse's back.

The thing was done in the old Bowery Theatre in New York City in the '50's. Levi J. North, who was performing in an opposition theatre, heard of the accomplishment and successfully imitated it the same night. John Glenroy followed with a somersault—performed without the presence of the pad then in general use and which his predecessors had alighted upon. Then James Robinson, creator of many bareback tricks, duplicated the act. Charles Fish, Frank Pastor, Romeo Sebastian and David Richards were other celebrated circus horsemen of that period. Billy Morgan inaugurated the now common mule riding act.

Mrs. Walter Howard was the first circus equestrienne of public prominence. Sixty years ago, her simple performance fairly dazed spectators. She gave lessons in her art to many of the later woman riders and made a sensation by being the only woman at that time to cast herself through paper balloons. Alice Lake was a remarkably skilful horsewoman. Of the foreigners who came here, Madame Tounaire was easily the best performer. Her daughter, Molly Brown, was the first woman in this country to somersault on a horse, and few women since have accomplished the trick. Mrs. William Roland, Madame Dockrill, Adelaide Cordona, Louise Rentz, and Pauline Lee attained prominence. Linda Jeal was famous for several years and taught her niece, Dallie Julian, seventeen years old, the somersault.

CHAPTER XVII

THE CIRCUS PRESS AGENT

The wily press agent's method of gaining publicity for his show varies with the size and moral disposition of the cities in which he finds himself. In executing his publicity-provoking designs in populous centres there is in him no serious purpose to avoid an arrest. In the smaller cities he must needs exercise his ingenuity to prevent the action of the law. The notion that showmen are moral delinquents is firmly settled in rural communities, especially in the East, and if in the excess of his enthusiasm to bring to wide attention the presence of the circus the press agent commits what an obdurate policeman considers a public wrong, and there follows an appearance before a magistrate, resentful townspeople look on him and his companions as lawbreaking intruders, rudely defying the local government, disturbing the peace, and ready, perhaps, to commit some more flagrant offence. A clergyman may make the incident a text of protest. It is bound anyway to arouse animosity and have a calamitous effect.

But in New York, Chicago, Boston, Philadelphia and cities approaching them in character and size, the standing of the circus is affected neither one way nor the other by an ingenuously-explained legal interruption, and the notice it attracts if it has unusual features shows gratifyingly at the box office. It isn't always easy to accomplish the thing. "Splash" Austin, whose first name, Paul, was a boyhood memory, was the high diver with one of the big circuses. He performed for the free edification of the crowd which gathered on the lot after the parade, which is the side-show harvest time. Later he was one of the features of the show itself. "Splash" was always at the press agent's service. The circus arrived in Chicago on Sunday for a week stand, and the press agent was ready with an elaborately planned venture. He and his aquatic accomplice drove to Lincoln Park bridge, where, by a coincidence which is not remarkable, a band of newspaper men were in waiting. The performer shed a few garments and plunged headforemost from the railing's height into the water. The feat was a simple one to the skilled acrobat, but its appearance was hazardous and spectacular, and the reporters marvelled and interviewed at length.

The beaming press agent's ingenuity had not been exhausted. Two frowning policemen intervened. Their pockets, the press agent alone knew, bulged with circus tickets. They were accommodatingly indignant; the law had been violated. "Splash" was put under arrest, and the party started in a body for the station house. On the way, the delighted author of the proceeding secured permission from "Splash's" captors to stop at a drink dispensary. The bluecoats waited outside while the circus man entertained. All were thirsty and happy, and the newspaper guests, in their innocence, cheerful over the unexpectedly "good" story which had developed. They have never known they tarried so long that one of the policemen called their host outside and whispered that there must be haste, two posts had been left vacant too long already, and they were half inclined to throw up the whole thing.

The day was eminently successful from the circus standpoint. The newspapers told at great length of the accomplishment of the daring dive and its tragic ending, and the public curiosity to see the performer added materially to receipts. And best of all none of the reporters was so wanting in human charity as to reveal that, at the police station, the captain had refused to hold the prisoner, remarking grimly that no offence had been committed; and that the press agent, searching frantically through the book of ordinances that his scheme not miscarry at the end, had found that a penalty attached to the crime of disturbing the fish in the lake, and patient "Splash" was locked up on that charge. A small fine was promptly paid next day.

FAIR EQUESTRIENNE ON HER FAVORITE HORSE.

Read one press agent's circus literature and begin to understand that the resources of the language are less limited than you suppose. He is the world-renowned alliterator of the show business. He is better known in the profession than Shakespeare, although Shakespeare never did much for circuses. He has no acknowledged rival in the successive use of the initial letter. The advance matter which he sends abroad for his "moral" enterprises where presumably only moral people are admitted, forms an extraordinary narrative.

During each winter he writes, writes, writes, writes, whether he feels right or not, but the annual incessant drain does not subtract from his elaborate eloquence. He tells of "real and royal races for reward, huge heroic hippodromes, genuine contests of strength, skill and speed, superb struggles for success and supremacy between the short and the stout, the tall and the tiny, the fat and the frail, the mammoth and the midget, the adipose and the attenuate, the large and the little, the massive and the minute, the swift and the slow; elephants in ponderous, pachydermic progress, camels in cross and comical cantering, horses in hurricane hustling for home, donkeys in deliberate, dragging, droning pace, monkeys in merry meanderings on meek and mild mules, whippets in whirlwind dashes swifter than a horse, runners in record reducing running in rivalry, ponies in carts with clowns for conductors, and the celebrated charioteer contestants of the Coliseum."

Proceeding in his product, after this gaudy prologue, this adjective-millionaire is impressed with the "astral array of aerial artists. The very air is filled with their flying forms, describing the most intricate figures, far flights, swallow-like sweeps, gymnic gyrations, castings and catches, revolutions and returns, swings and somersaults, leapings and lightnings, soarings and sailings, altitudinous ascensions, diving descensions, keeping the dizzy heights of the lofty canvas dome alive with activity. Never before have the satiated public seen a spectacle to so surely stir their sluggish blood, arouse their admiration, excite their enthusiasm and command their applause."

The clowns appeal to him. As phrased by him they are "a phenomenal phalanx of phantastical, phuriously phunny phellows; silly and sedate, short and stout, smile securers set scot free; loyal legion of long and lean laugh liberators let loose. These extraordinary experts in the creation of laughter have invented this year a new, novel, unique, irresistibly comic, excruciatingly funny and simply surprising series of skits, scenes, screaming sallies and silly situations."

Danger is "defiantly defied by one audacious aerial athlete, whose deed is daring, desperate and death deriding, a fearless, fearful, fascinating feat, the veritable pinnacle of perillous performances."

"Whirling Wonders of the World on Wheels" are "cycling champions in clubs and coteries, in single, double and tandem teams, in wheeling fads, fancy and freakish, in pictorial and picturesque peripatetic posturings."

Proceeding, he describes the elephants as "mountains in motion, ponderous and perspicacious pachyderms, in marvellous, military manoeuvres."

The districts remote from New York are assured that "every element and entity that enthused, excited and enthralled in the enormous Madison Square Garden will be a part and parcel of the prodigious performance." And as a "super-splendid spectacular suggestion of greater, grander glories yet to come, early in the forenoon of the day of exhibition there will pass through the principal streets of the city the most mammoth, monster mass of moving magnificence that ever fell athwart the delighted, gratified, entranced vision of the human eye, the nearly all new free street parade, including an interesting and instructive illustration of the progress of our glorious Republic, showing in correct uniform the soldiers of all American wars; gorgeous tableaux, many massive, open dens, glittering cavalcades of knights and ladies, representatives of the regiment of Roosevelt's Rough Riders, comic clowns and grotesque grimaldis, rollicking rubes and jolly jays, herds of ponderous elephants, droves of camels, floods of music from military bands, etc., etc."

"Some circus owners never appreciate the valuable services we render them," lamented a veteran press agent who has toured two continents under a tent. "The ignominious end of my graveyard specialty is an example of the palpable lack of sentiment and business astuteness sometimes disclosed when one least expects it. I observed that almost every town has turned upon the public a circus man of high or low degree, who finally returns to his native spot to pass his last days and be put away in the local cemetery. With the arrival of the circus his career becomes a topic of conversation among the townsfolk and invariably newspaper reporter, hotel keeper or some other resident engaged me in talk about the man. I always unblushingly remembered him vividly and was able, after a few leading questions, to shed much entertaining light upon his circus life, to express well-feigned surprise that the body of so well-known a character was buried there and to express a deep feeling of sorrow over the loss the profession had sustained in his death. Sometimes I would urge the erection of a more suitable monument and reproach townspeople for their neglect.

"Not infrequently the subject of my solicitude had been a four-horse driver, a trombone player or a stake driver. But his professional insignificance was not appreciated by the friends of his life time, my tender expressions made good feelings toward the show, and I let no opportunity pass ungrasped. Sometimes the newspapers quoted my sentiments, and it helped business.

"If I had only been content with my own perfidious eloquence I wouldn't have got disgusted and quit. But I was ambitious and wanted to throw away no chance to boom the show. So, soon, in every town in which I could locate an appropriate headstone, I put on black clothes, a countenance of becoming sadness and marched the band to the graveyard. They played dirges all the way. Frank Morris, the orator of the circus, accompanied us and I had him make an address at the grave. I wrote out three non-committal speeches and there was no dead man whose life didn't fit one or judiciously selected parts of the three. They were all very affecting, and made the women cry. On the way back to the lot we always got a loving ovation. The newspapers spoke approvingly of the proceedings and the residents thought it a great compliment. I was very proud of myself.

"The thing went along swimmingly for several weeks and my motives were never openly assailed, although I think once or twice there lurked a suspicion in the minds of shrewd townspeople that their departed brother wasn't all in life that we represented him. Anyway, I know it brought money to the circus, and I could never understand the boss's secret disapproval. He never offered any sensible, legitimate objection, but I could tell by his manner that he was afraid of some kind of a boomerang finish some day. I persevered aggressively, nevertheless, and was confident he would never get a valid excuse for forbidding us to continue. I knew the experienced old man of affairs was waiting warily for a chance.

"The success or failure of the concert depended in a great measure upon Morris's oratory. When in good voice and spirits, he could fairly glue his auditors to their seats. They wouldn't budge until they had seen all the concert attractions about which he had so insinuatingly roared. So it was through him that the boss found opportunity to base a complaint, put an end to my practices and lower my estimate of his business intelligence. One unlucky day Morris caught a bad cold. He was hoarse and depressed, and his announcement was received with little favor. The concert attendance was small and the head of the show was quick to seize his advantage—and strike at my burying-ground plot.

"'Morris got that cold in one of your graveyards,' he addressed me, reproachfully, 'and we'll have to give him a rest from this double duty. Let those fellows rest in peace in their graves after this!'

"I left the show a month later, disgusted and discouraged, and found a place where my fine art received support and confidence and gratitude."

In the Southern States several years ago a circus now disorganized was in high popular favor, and it was with great difficulty and at heavy expense that the "big shows" of to-day succeeded in convincing the population that its confidence had been misplaced. Finally, however, they were welcomed and accepted. The colored public was the last to forsake its cherished tradition.

An advance press agent strolling past the flaring billboards announcing the approach to an Alabama town of the metropolitan organization he represented, observed an aged, tottering darkey, supported by a small boy of his race. They were scrutinizing the posters.

"Read it to me, son," directed the old man. "What dey say about dis new circus?"

The lad stared ruefully at the polysyllabic collection and began slowly: "Of all magnificent and master consolidations of rare, varied and illustrious menageries, circus and hippodrome possessions and possibilities this is greatest. Sept. 1, ——."

"Dat's enough, my boy, dat's enough," interrupted the attentive old listener, shaking his head grimly and chuckling, "'cept one, eh, 'cept one. I know dat one. It's de circus I's been seein' for years. Dis false show don't git none ob my money."

A free ticket, produced on the spot, helped to shake his faith, but history does not record whether the performance made him a thorough convert.

Adam Forepaugh was as ready a man in an emergency as circus life ever developed, and was noted in the business for his skill in avoiding legal entanglements. A resident of Auburn, N. Y., does not know to this day how neatly the showman escaped a claim for damages at his expense. The man had been drinking heavily, and in the menagerie tent before the performance had begun offered Bolivar, an elephant noted for his size, a bottle filled with whiskey. The smell of the liquid always infuriates the beasts. In the spring of 1902, Tops, a usually good-natured elephant, stamped the life out of a man who offended her with whiskey, in Brooklyn, N. Y. The Auburn man was chased away unharmed by the watchful keepers, but Bolivar's small eyes gleamed vindictively and he did not forget. The performance was well under way, and the menagerie tent was being rapidly emptied of its collection of animals and cages, when the man returned. The elephants and camels were lined up preparatory to the march to the cars. The scene was one of confusion and excitement, and the man was not observed by the attendants. Bolivar, however, had his eyes fixed on his persecutor and as the luckless stranger came within reach the big beast trumpeted, struck with his trunk and prepared to stamp upon the victim. Keepers rushed to the spot with pitchforks, subdued the angry elephant and dragged the unconscious form away. An examination showed no serious injury.

Visions of a sheriff, attachment and suit for heavy damages oppressed Mr. Forepaugh at once, but his quick wit suggested a way out of the trouble.

"Take this fellow to the cars," he shouted to "Dan" Taylor, boss canvasman, "and keep him locked there. Don't let him out when he gets his senses again, but bring him to me in the morning in Syracuse."

The bruised and wondering man was taken like a prisoner, according to instructions, before the owner of the show next day. Mr. Forepaugh's attitude was that of a judge on the police court bench. A withering frown was on his face.

"You're a nice specimen to hire out as a driver," he observed severely, "you were so drunk you fell off the wagon. You are discharged. I can't tolerate intoxication with my circus. It's fortunate you were not killed and the horses didn't run away."

The effects of drink and the blow he received had driven memory from the unfortunate man's brain, and as Mr. Forepaugh perceived it a load was lifted from him. He talked kindly but firmly to the penitent before him, dwelt on the evils of intemperance and finally offered him a day's pay if he would promise not to drink liquor for a year. The pledge was solemnly given and, I have been told, the man was ever after consecrated to sobriety.

A good story is told by a former press agent of one of the big circuses of how Samuel D. Clemens (Mark Twain) was out-humored at his home in Hartford, Conn., by an untutored savage. The enterprising agent decided it would be a good advertisement to get an interview between Mr. Clemens and one of the Indians who were then a feature of the show. He called on the humorist and laid the matter before him. Mr. Clemens said that he didn't care for the Indians, he was very busy, and didn't see what Indians had to do with him, anyway.

"Why, the fact is," replied the circus man, "they have heard of you in the far West and want to see you."

Still Mr. Clemens was indisposed to grant the request until the press agent swore solemnly that a big Sioux Chief had said that he would never die happy, if compelled to return to his reservation without seeing and speaking with the man whose fame was world-wide.

"All right," finally assented the humorist. "Have him here at six o'clock this evening, but make it short."

Mr. Clemens sat on the broad porch of his home in Farmington avenue at the appointed time. The house was a fine, long, rambling red brick structure standing near the top of a green breezy hill. To the astonishment of the man he perceived an immense cavalcade of mounted warriors, more than half a hundred of them, tearing along the broad, airy boulevard in a mad exhibition of horsemanship. They swept in on the lawn, breaking down the shrubbery, wearing off the grass and devastating the whole place like a destroying army. A crowd of boys were at their heels, trampling flower beds and shrubs. The spokesman of the party was a mighty hunter who had been previously told that Mark Twain was famous for his slaughter of wild beasts.

The Indian laid himself out for a game of brag. The interpreter, who was in the deal, instead of repeating what the chief said, made a speech of his own, extolling Twain's literary achievements.

"For Heaven's sake, choke him off!" ejaculated the sad funny-man, with blanched face. The cracking of boughs in the choice trees in which the small boys had ensconced themselves were punctuating the Indian's remarks.

The interpreter turned to the red man and soberly remarked that the White Hunter wanted more talk, and on he went. Every time Twain cried for quarter the chief was told to give another hunting story. Finally his Indian vocabulary was exhausted and he quit.

Twain made a brief reply which the interpreter translated into a marvellous hunting yarn. The Chief listened stolidly, and when he got away grunted contemptuously and muttered:

"White man heap big liar."

Adam Forepaugh, in the latter years of his circus life, carried with his show a "Wild West" department. He had Indians, cowboys, Mexicans, Cossacks, Arabs, scouts, guides, detachments of regular soldiers from the armies of several nations and all the others that go to make a spectacular rough-riding production. I remember an amusing incident which illustrates that the veteran tented-amusement purveyor did not allow sentiment to interfere with the ticket wagon end of the business. One of the features of the exhibition was a representation of Custer's disastrous battle with the Sioux Indians under Sitting Bull. The *mise en scène* was correct in most particulars, and carried out with fidelity to the subject. It was a graphic illustration of the Indian mode of warfare. The cowboys who participated were true children of the plains who had faced danger in many of its deadliest forms. They were very proud of their records as scouts, plainsmen and warriors.

Along about the middle of the season Mr. Forepaugh picked up a famous addition to the show in Mt. Vernon, O. He was Sergeant George C. Wagner, "representative frontiersman of the past." He came unannounced, looking for a job in the Wild West department, hopping on to the lot like a clumsy bird. A wooden prop replaced the flesh and bone of his right leg below the knee. He explained to Mr. Forepaugh that he was the sole survivor of Custer's immediate command; he had escaped death in the last rally, because at the time of the fight he was riding the plains with a message to Major Reno, seventy-two miles away. During his lonely journey he had encountered Indians, and a poisoned arrow received in the running conflict had necessitated amputation of his leg. He looked the figure of romance and adventure, impressed the circus owner as sincere and was hired on the spot.

ACROBATS PRACTISING NEW FEATS.

As the days went by the sergeant became more and more a conspicuous part of the show. He was a skilful horseman, despite his abbreviated limb, although we all wondered how he was able to hold his seat. His name appeared in black type on the programme, and he always got a tremendous ovation when he scurried on a big bay horse around the hippodrome amid the blare of trumpets, after a highly complimentary introduction by the announcer. After the show, Grand Army posts frequently gave him informal receptions, at which he regaled the veterans with thrilling stories of life on the trail and of incidents of the excitement and turmoil of the unsettled West. He drank whiskey with great freedom and frequency, but it seemed to affect only his tongue. His encounters with red men then became innumerable and his life history was written all over with blood. His knowledge of Custer's campaigns was comprehensive to a detail.

Mr. Forepaugh was mightily pleased with the acquisition, but not so the cowboys, the true sons of the frontier. All the honors of the show were Wagner's and they were jealous. One day one of them suggested a systematic review of their gallant comrade's past in the hope of uncovering an act of cowardice or crime, and the proposition met general favor. They hired a lawyer to investigate and his report was received in a surprisingly short time. The man who had represented himself as cradled amid pioneer surroundings had never been out of the Ohio county in which he revealed himself until the circus adopted him, and he had lost his leg by a premature anvil explosion at a Fourth of July celebration.

It was at this juncture that Adam Forepaugh lost, in a great measure, the respect and admiration of the cowboy fraternity, and proved, as I have observed, that noble emotions and lofty ideals cannot always rise supreme in the circus business. The cowboys, with many strange oaths and threats, presented their damning narrative, confident that the hour of retribution was at hand and that the owner of the show would express sympathy and gratitude for the disclosure. Wagner, they thought, would be clubbed off the lot.

Mr. Forepaugh listened intently to the story of the imposition. He, too, I know, had been as thoroughly deceived as the rest of us, but he wasn't willing the show should suffer.

"What do I care," he remarked quickly, and the expectant faces of the cowboys blanched, "whether the fellow's a fakir or not? He looks the part better than any of you, he's got a wooden leg to confirm it, he's the finest liar under the tent and he's made a big hit. He stays with the troupe."

"Sergeant" Wagner continued as hero, guide, and scout until the season's close, when he disappeared and the Wild West department heard of him no more. The memory of his dare-devil appearance, long golden locks floating in the wind, wide sombrero, buckskin breeches and protruding guns will not be effaced for many years.

The gnawing fear of attachments is never absent from the circus owner's mind, and with all his mental wealth of resource, acquired by hard experience, he cannot always escape imposition. The sheriff becomes an object of hate and dread. His appearance with a levy, the showman knows, is a portend of extortion. So it is that sometimes he submits to injustice rather than bring about a conflict with the law. Unscrupulous people appreciate this, with its fine opportunity for blackmail, but sometimes the instigator comes as a shock and a surprise to the circus owner and helps to shake his faith in the general honest impulses accredited to human nature.

We were playing the Ohio towns. Business was big, weather fine and everybody was happy. One day a negro preacher, hat in hand and apologetic in manner, approached the owner and explained a grievance. His church edifice, eight miles outside the town, had been posted with our glaring show bills, the congregation was angry and mortified and threatening to go over in a body to another parish, and the church receipts had fallen to nothing. One hundred dollars would set things right. A lawyer who fingered a bunch of legal papers ominously was with the outraged clergyman. The circus compromised for fifty dollars and got a release.

We showed next day in a town fourteen miles distant. Before the parade had formed, the colored minister of the day before again confronted us. He was humble and devout enough in appearance, but the same lawyer was his companion, and a man whom we knew was the sheriff hovered on the outskirts of the lot. The man of religion lamented his complaint of the preceding day without a variation, and concluded the narrative again with a demand for pecuniary balm.

"Why, I settled with you yesterday," the astonished owner retorted. "I gave you fifty dollars, and hold your paper of satisfaction. You have no further claim."

"You see, Mr. Circus man," was the ready answer, "my church is on the county line. Yesterday you paid for desecrating the house of God in Lorain county. But you also profaned our sacred worshipping place in Cuyahoga county. I want damages now for the actual and religious injury done there."

If we hadn't been so prosperous, I know the owner wouldn't have yielded. As it was, the unblushing effrontery of the thing appealed to his sense of humor, and he gave the man another fifty dollars. He told of the proceeding at dinner as a good joke at his expense, and remarked that, after all, he was not sorry to have had the chance to contribute to the finances of the struggling congregation. It might bring him good luck.

About three o'clock in the afternoon he told me to ascertain the whereabouts of the church—he had become curious about the shrewd preacher's affairs—and we would drive out there. The church was about six miles away, through a lonely country district. We lost our way once and the circus owner was not in the best of humor when we arrived. The sight that greeted him knocked out all the exalted sentiment that had stirred him. The steeple of the building was on a level with the eaves, two cows browsed off the pulpit, there was evidence of the nocturnal presence of hens in the amen corner, and the whole edifice was in a state of dilapidation and decay. Along the entire front was an inch and a half accumulation of circus bills. Ours were the outside strata. The minister couldn't be found, fortunately for his physical welfare. He was probably spending his booty. His wife told us the congregation had dissolved months ago, and our adroit questioning disclosed that the couple's income consisted in a great measure of the money extracted from the circuses who, innocently, utilized the inviting stretch of ecclesiastical boards. The memory of the colored clergyman is still green with the circus man, and religion is at a discount with the show.

P. T. Barnum, in the early years of his life, had no modern press agent, but it is doubtful if the interesting person could have aided the showman in advertising his enterprises. No one knew better than he the value of printer's ink, and of the men who made printer's ink the vehicle of news and information. Old circus men recall an illustration of his unique but impressive way of attracting public attention in 1849, which would have done credit to this enlightened generation. He sent an expedition to Ceylon, a formidable undertaking then, to capture elephants. They returned to New York with ten of the animals, harnessed them in pairs to a chariot and drove up Broadway. Not content with this advertisement, he sent one of the elephants to his Connecticut farm and engaged the beast in agricultural pursuits. A keeper, clad in oriental costume, was the companion. They were stationed on a six-acre lot which lay close beside the tracks of the New York and New Haven railroad. The keeper was furnished with a timetable of the road with special instructions to be busily engaged in plowing, with the animal dragging the implement, whenever passenger trains passed. The proceeding made a sensation and the showman gravely announced that he intended to introduce a herd of elephants to do all his plowing and heavy draft work. After the six acres had been plowed over at least a hundred times, he quietly returned the animal to his museum.

It is related in the circus world that the "Feejee Mermaid" was the stepping-stone to Barnum's road to wealth and circus renown. The thing was made in Japan with an ingenuity and mechanical perfection well calculated to deceive. Barnum bought it in 1842, when he was unknown, modified by printer's ink the general incredulity as to the possibility of the existence of mermaids, and aroused great curiosity to see and examine his specimen. Then, too, he persuaded some naturalist to endorse it as genuine. The fame of his museum and its preserved curiosity was wafted from one end of the land to the other. Money flowed in rapidly and the notoriety he attained he never permitted to fade.

In the museum, the ladder by which he rose to fortune, Mr. Barnum a few months later perpetrated another humbug which arrested public attention. He purchased in Cincinnati, O., a well-formed, small-sized horse, with no mane and not a particle of hair on his tail, while his body and legs were covered with thick, fine hair or wool, which curled tight to his skin. The animal had been foaled in Ohio and was a remarkable freak of nature. The astute showman immediately advertised the beast as "The Woolly Horse." The news had just come that Colonel John C. Fremont, who was supposed to have been lost in the snows of the Rocky Mountains, was in safety. Mr. Barnum grasped the opportunity and asserted that his horse had been captured by the explorer's party. The curiosity was a great attraction for many months, and no definite exposure of the imposition was ever made. It added immeasurably to the reputation and pecuniary success of the establishment.

The circus press agent is a welcome visitor to the country newspaper office. In his gratitude over the influx of tickets and advertising, the editor generally devotes space to a eulogy of the social and professional merits of the visitor. Here are some truthfully reproduced specimens, taken at random from a collection:

"The bustling press agent of the vast concourse is the most popular man with the circus."

"The press agent is built for a gentleman from the ground up, and he acts it with the ease and dignity of a Chesterfield."

"The management is fortunate in having for its press representative ———, who is a gentleman in every way, and who understands his business thoroughly."

"The press agent is one of the most genial gentlemen in the profession, and he is much liked by the newspapers wherever he goes, not only because he is liberal with the pasteboards, but because he is a hale fellow well met."

"——— leaves nothing undone on his part to make the grand show popular."

"——— is a mighty clever gentleman. He called at our office to-day and made himself agreeable."

"The press agent of the circus is undoubtedly an element of strength in that big institution. He is a mighty pleasant gentleman and knows exactly how to make himself popular with the newspaper men."

"He is the right man in the right place."

"The show has four aces in ———, the press representative, who is such a thorough gentleman that his kindness to the press boys issues his own patent to nobility."

"The press agent treated us nicely yesterday. Several little attentions he gave us made us feel more than kind to him."

"The circus is lucky in having him for press agent. He is a refined and courteous gentleman to whom much is due for the success and popularity of this great show."

"The press of this section will always welcome the coming of this genial gentleman."

"But probably the most versatile artist of this great aggregation was ———, the press agent of this enormous aggregation. He deserves special mention."

"On last Thursday evening of the circus, the editor of the ———, upon invitation of the pleasing and wide awake press agent, went 'behind the scenes' on a tour of the dressing-rooms of the great institution. We were first introduced to the great and only ———, just preparing to mount the twenty-three bareback horses, which he rides to the consternation of all who see him. Going to the left, the curtain was raised and Trunktown was seen, that is, about one hundred and fifty people sitting upon, diving into, standing or beside their trunks, in various stages of dishabille, preparing for their various acts. Taking off his plug, the press agent announced the presence of the editor, and everybody came forward and shook us by the hand—for a little while we thought we were running for President of the United States. A chair was brought for us and a little chat indulged in with those near, among whom was the great bareback rider. We had a chat with the gladiators, also, who were making up for their act, one of the most pleasing and artistic of the show. In shaking hands with those chaps we got some white powder on our left shoulder, which they use to powder their faces. After returning to our wife in the circus auditorium, we had great difficulty in explaining the powder away. But the press agent bore testimony that we had not visited the ladies' dressing-rooms, not being the right gender."

An old-time press agent, writing a brief list of a few men met with in the circus's transitory career and who will continue to exist when showmen of this generation have passed on, mentions:

The man who travelled with Dan Rice.

The man who when a boy carried water for the elephant.

The man who knew the man who sold his cook stove to secure the price of a circus ticket.

The man who knows how many thousands of dollars the circus takes out of town.

The man who is anxious to know when "show folks" sleep.

The man who sympathizes with us because of our "hard life."

The man who asks: "Where do you go from here?"

The man who knows the show is "split up" in the smaller towns.

The man who is sure "this is the best show town of its size in the United States."